ARCHAEOLOGY
IN THE LAND
OF THE BIBLE

ARCHAEOLOGY IN THE LAND OF THE BIBLE

AVRAHAM NEGEV

SCHOCKEN BOOKS · NEW YORK

CONTRIBUTORS

Prof. Avraham Negev

Professor of Classical Archaeology,
The Hebrew University of Jerusalem

Assistance in Picture Research
Irene Lewitt
Editorial Assistance Ronny Stein
Design & Layout Yishai Afek
First published by SCHOCKEN BOOKS 1977
Copyright © 1976 SADAN Publishing House Ltd.
P.O.B. 16096. Tel Aviv. Israel
Manufactured in Israel

Library of Congress Cataloging in Publication Data

Negev, Avraham.
  Archaeology in the land of the Bible.

  1. Palestine — Antiquities. 2. Bible — Antiquities.
3. Excavations (Archaeology) — Palestine. I. Title.
DS111.N38 1977   933   77-23213

Jacket Illustration
Aerial view of Masada; the excavations in this major archaeological
site uncover the glory of King Herod's period, his sumptuous
palaces and fortifications and reveals the story of the great Jewish
revolt against the Romans. Masada marks the end of the Jewish
national independence.

Back Cover
The Isaiah scroll, discovered at the Qumran caves, to the shore of
the Dead Sea, forms an important part of the biblical books, copied
by the scribes of the small sect who lived there in sanctity, and which
antedated by 1,000 years any other extant copy of the Bible.

Titlepage
"The Sacrifice of Isaac".
Fragment of the mosaic floor at the synagogue of Beth Alpha. 6th
century AD.

Endpapers
Relief from the palace of Sennacherib at Nineveh, depicting the
battle on Lachish, on the eve of the fall of Jerusalem and the exile of
Judah. 7th century BC.

ACKNOWLEDGEMENTS
The publishers wish to thank the following for permission to reproduce illustrations (Numbers refer to sequence of photographs):
The Department of Antiquities, Israel Ministry of Education and Culture: 3, 5, 6, 8, 9, 10, 11, 12, 13, 14, 15, 19, 20, 21, 22, 23, 25, 26, 27, 28, 29, 30, 31,
32, 33, 34, 36, 38, 46, 47, 48, 51, 52, 56, 57, 58, 61, 76, 95, 97, 102, 108, 117, 118, 121, 125, 126, XX, XXII, XXVI, XXVII, XXXVII. The
Archaeological Institute, the Hebrew University of Jerusalem: 2, 35. The Hebrew Union College: 18, 39. Prof. Ygael Yadin; first published in his books
"Hazor II":24, "Tefilin from Qumran": 87, XXXII. The Albright Institute, Jerusalem: 40. The Archaeological Institute, Tel Aviv University: 44, 45. The
Israel Exploration Society, Jewish Quarter Excavations: 60, 64, 65, 66, 67, 69, 70, 72. The Israel Exploration Society, Western Wall Excavations: 66, 68,
73, 74, 75, 100. The Israel Exploration Society: XXXIV. Archaeological Museum of Istanbul: 50, 55. Bessin Collection: 49, 59. Reifenberg Collection
80, 82. Museum Ha'aretz, Tel Aviv: 42, 43. Israel Museum, the Shrine of the Book: 85, 86, 87, 88, 89, 91, 92, 93. After E. L. Sukenik "The Ancient
Synagogue of Beth Alpha", Jerusalem, 1932: XXXI. Holyland Hotel, Jerusalem: XXXI. The Library of the Hague: XXXVII. The Haifa Music
Museum XXVIII. Jerusalem City Museum: XXXVIII. H. H. McWilliams: XXV. National Maritime Museum, Haifa: XXI. Kadman Numismatic
Museum, Tel Aviv XXX. Rijksmuseum van Oudheden, Leiden: VIII.
and to the following for providing photographs:
Israel Museum — photo D. Harris: 6, 8, 9, 10, 11, 21, 22, 23, 33, 34, 46, 47, 48, 49, 55, 57, 61, 82, 93, 104, V. Israel Museum — photo H. Burger 5, 20,
26, 28, 29, 31, 32, 118, XXXVII. Israel Museum — photo N. Bareket 52, 97. G. Nalbandian 1, 17, 25, 53, 62, 63, 94, 96, 101, 103, 109, 112, 122, 123,
124. Z. Radovan: 35, 64, VII, XVI, XXIII. Kathleen Kenyon: 4. W. Braun: 37, 71, 77, 84, 115, 120, 127. A. Hay: 42, 43, 44. D. Barag: 106, 107. R.
Brody: 130. D. Darom: 128. D. Harris: 7, 30, 36, 38, 50, 54, 58, 108, 131, XII. N. Bareket: 90. Israel Government Press Office: 98, 99, 105, 113.
National Fund of Israel: 110. Fr. Delfin Fernandez: 119. R. Kneller: 78, front-cover. Israel Museum: 12, 13, 14, 15, 34, 41, 59, 80, 85, 86, 87, 91, 92.

★ City mentioned in sources to map;   ◉ Capital;   • Trial excavation or minor remains;   △ Excavation;

▲ Major excavation; Names in parentheses are non-contemporary or modern.   Errata: p.95 Pilatus; p.120 Oboda.

ARCHAEOLOGY IN THE LAND OF THE BIBLE

Archaeology, the scientific study of the material remains of the past, is one of the most ancient of sciences. Greek Mythology is, in fact, one very early expression of it; the Romans were themselves in the habit of collecting Greek antiquities, of which they made copies. In the Hellenistic period old books were collected in libraries, and the Jewish historian Josephus Flavius named his book *Jewish Archaeology.* When the Bible was codified many of the ancient cities mentioned in it had already long since vanished without trace. But as their identification was of importance in matters of religious law, attempts were made by the sages of the *Mishnah* and the *Talmud,* the Jewish oral law, to locate these sites. These sages knew quite well that virgin soil does not contain sherds. The identification of ancient sites troubled no less the Fathers of the Christian Church, and the *Onomasticon* of Eusebius is still one of the most important sources for the study of the ancient topography of the Land of the Bible.

In many cases archaeology provides the only evidence of the material and spiritual state of ancient cultures. This is certainly true of the vast period of prehistory, and holds good for some historic times as well. The first millenia of the historic period left some written records, but it is only by the finds of daily life that a better picture may be obtained of the complexity of ancient human existence. Though the Holy Land is a rather poor country in comparison with the richer surrounding empires, it has nevertheless gained a very prominent place in archaeological research. It occupies a comparatively narrow strip along the Mediterranean coast, bordering on deserts to the south and the east, the endless sea to the west and fertile Syria to the north. Despite its small dimensions two of the most important ancient international trade routes traversed it — the *Via Maris* along the coast on the west, and the King's Highway along the Transjordanian plateau on the east. These two much frequented routes connected the northern empires with Egypt and with fabulous Arabia. Because of its strategic importance the Holy Land has been the object of numerous conquerors and the scene of countless battles in times of war, and an artery of international cultural interchange by way of commerce in times of peace. All of these activities left more than a passing trace in the archaeology of the Holy Land.

The fact that this has been the Land of the Bible is the main cause of its attraction for hosts of archaeologists of various nationalties. The 24 books of the

Canaanite man and woman painted on pottery sherds. Beth Shean. Late Canaanite period.

Bible contain the laws by which the Chosen People lived, their history from the remote past to their return from the Babylonian exile, the exhortations of their prophets and some of their best religio-literary compositions. These books not only became the heritage of later Judaism, but also formed the solid foundation on which the other two major monotheistic religions, Christianity and Islam, were built. As such, the Bible formed the basis of countless studies, some aiming to achieve a better understanding of the spiritual meaning of the Scriptures, while others aspired to a clearer picture of everyday life, or of a particular historical event and its relation to the history of the surrounding peoples. The actual route of the Exodus and the search for remains of the conquest of Canaan by the tribes of Israel are only two of the numerous questions which challenge and inspire the archaeologist. What would we have known of the material culture of the Philistines were it not for the results of archaeological research?

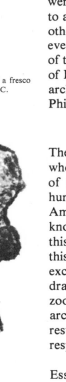

Head of Semite, part of a fresco at Mari. 18th century BC.

The limited scope of this book makes it impossible to mention all the scholars to whom we are indebted for our knowledge of the subject. During the two centuries of modern archaeological research the Holy Land has been investigated by hundreds of scholars, British, French, German, Danish, Italian, Japanese, American, Israeli, to mention only a few nationalities at random. Our present knowledge is a synthesis of the contributions of all these scholars, some active at this stage of research, others in the past. Good archaeology is team work, and this is true even in the case of a small-scale archaeological excavation. No excavation can be done without the manual laborer, the recorder, the draughtsman, architect, photographer, epigraphist, numismatist, botanist, zoologist, to mention only a few, on whose co-operation the success of an archaeological excavation depends. The archaeologist is a coordinator of the results of the work of each of the participants in his specific field of interest, responsible for the proper interpretation and publication of this combined effort.

Essentially the Holy Land has been part of the sown lands, although it bordered geographically on a desert which now comprises half of the territory of present day Israel. Researches made by the present author during the past two decades in the Negev region, have shown that it did not follow the same rules which underlay the development of settlement in the region north of Beersheba, nor did it share a common history. It is for this reason that I have limited the description of this region.

THE PREHISTORIC PERIOD

The first forebears of human culture set foot on the tiny strip of earth later known as the Holy Land about a million years ago. It is, however, only in the very recent past that archaeology has begun to illuminate the obscure life of prehistoric man.

Some 250,000 years before our time man in the Holy Land began his long and arduous way toward a settled life. During most of this period stone was the chief material with which he fashioned tools and weapons — hence the period is designated the Stone Age. The Stone Age may be subdivided into Old, Middle and New Stone Age depending on certain changes in the material culture. Each of these long periods is further subdivided into shorter periods which derive their names from the region where they were first recognized.

THE OLD STONE AGE

During the early part of the Old Stone Age the Holy Land was a country of large lakes and rivers. At that time man lived in open-air shelters, in the vicinity of water sources, slowly penetrating into the mountaneous regions, finding shelter in natural caves. One of the most important sites of this cultural phase was discovered at Ubeidiya, south of the Sea of Galilee.

The middle phase of the Old Stone Age saw an increase in the number of cave dwellers, and remains of the more important prehistoric communities were discovered in caves on the western slopes of Mount Carmel, in the Galilee, and in other parts of the country. The man of this cultural phase incorporated characteristics of the European Neanderthal and the more developed *Homo Sapiens*. This type has been named *Palaeanthropus Palestinensis* — Ancient Palestinian Man. Recently developed dating techniques help to date this type to about 35,000 years before our time.

At a later phase of this cultural stage the wet and hot climate which had stimulated the rapid expansion of the human race in the Holy Land, gave way to a more severe climatic regime. The cold and dry weather drove away the big game, food became scarcer, and man was forced to hunt smaller animals. The drying out of the rivers and lakes compelled man to find shelter in the caves, in open places closer to the Mediterranean coast, and in the vicinity of inland springs.

Part of an anthropomorphic pottery sarcophagus, from the Philistine necropolis at Beth Shean. 12th century BC.

During the later Old Stone Age several drastic cultural developments occurred over a comparatively short period of time. The man who lived in Palestina at this period is known as Aurignacian Man, after the place in France where his remains were first identified. The hardships of life, and scarcity of food, forced man to produce a new type of small implement (microliths) for hunting small animals and fish.

THE NATUFIAN CULTURE

At about 10,000 BC, the end of the Pleistocene — the last geological era — the Natufian culture made its appearance. This local culture is named after Wadi Natuf, northwest of Jerusalem, where the first finds were made. In terms of prehistory it was of a very short duration, lasting for a few thousand years only. At sites at which this culture was noted there occurs a vast diversity of new types and shapes of stone implements, and new materials for their production were also introduced. Among the stone implements has been found the pestle, attesting to the fact that man enriched his meat and fish diet with cereals, most probably obtained from wild growing corn. An analysis of the teeth of the Natufians shows a kind of wear which could only have been produced by the consumption of cereals.

One of the new materials which the Natufians introduced was bone. Not only were harpoons and handles of implements made of bone, but on it were made the first attempts at artistic and religious expression. We thus find figures of humans and animals, realistically represented, or in schematic, stylized form. Jewelery was also made of bone.

Semite captives and their Egyptian guard, from a Memphis relief. 14th century BC.

Some of the Natufians continued to live in caves, but there were also some small communities which preferred to live in round huts in the open. These huts consisted of a low socle made of field-stones, covered either by branches of trees or by hides. Remains of some communities were discovered in the vicinity of caves in which the ancestors of the Natufians lived; there also were Natufian settlements in the vicinity of the Hulah Valley in the north, and at Jericho in the south.

BURIAL.   All the Natufian settlements contained burial grounds. The Natufians were probably the first men who attached some importance to the disposal of the dead. Men were buried either singly or in communal graves. In the single graves the bodies were placed in certain prescribed positions — lying flat on their backs, contracted, or seated on their heels. In the communal graves — large holes excavated in the ground — the skulls and other bones were collected in separate heaps, and covered by heavy stones to prevent the disturbance of the bones for eternity. The foreheads, arms and hips of some of the dead, mainly women, were decorated by strings of beads. It thus seems obvious that the Natufians attached some cultic importance to the proper disposal of dead relatives. This ritual attitude toward death was obviously based on some vision of an after-life. The women were buried with bone necklaces around their heads. Great importance was attached to the fertility cult, indicating the Natufians' sense of being at the arbitary mercy of nature.

THE NEOLITHIC PERIOD
The Natufian culture lasted for about 2,000 years. At about 8,000 BC began the New Stone Age, which was a truly revolutionary period. Culturally it is divided into two separate periods, Pre-Pottery and Pottery Neolithic.

THE FIRST CITY.   By the beginning of the earlier phase, durirg the 8th millenium BC, a fortified city was built at Jericho, believed to be the earliest city in the world. This city, situated at the northern end of the Dead Sea, where the Jordan enters its waters, was defended by a wall and a massive round tower. Its dwellings consisted of socles of stone with superstructures of mud-bricks. This early city provides the most direct evidence that the men who populated the Holy Land at that time had taken the last step from nomadic and semi-nomadic life to that of permanent settlement.

The variety of stone tools and implements found at Jericho and other sites pertaining to this period included among the regular arrow-heads used in hunting and warfare a large number of sickle-blades and reaping knives. It was the transition from food-gathering to the production of food which caused Neolithic man to build towns and villages in the fertile and well-watered plains of the country.

To the same early Neolithic town of Jericho belongs also an oblong building, possibly a shrine, with clay figurines of men and animals related to some cult. Of much interest were a large number of human skulls found below the floors of dwellings. These were covered by soft clay, in which the features of the face were sculpted. These skulls may have belonged to an ancestral cult at Jericho. The city is indeed a wondrous achievement for so early a period as the 8th century BC. Rich evidence was found of a prosperous urban life and a well-organized society.

THE PRODUCTION OF POTTERY.   The foundation of a city, domestication of animals and the systematic planting of wild corn began well before pottery was produced. It was only in the later phases of the Neolithic period that the production of pottery began. The early pottery vessels were coarsely made, mostly hand-made large jars. The soft clay of which these vessels were molded provided their makers with another artistic medium, and indeed many of these primitive containers of water and grain, found at Jericho, Shaar Hagolan and other Pottery-Neolithic sites, have impressed and incised decorations

This transition to full sedenterization, symbolized by the introduction of pottery, was preceded at Jericho by the abandonment of the city, which was replaced by a small rural settlement, founded possibly by a different culture.

AGRICULTURE AND THE FERTILITY CULT.   On sites occupied during the Pottery-Neolithic period a large variety of implements connected with the tilling of the soil, such as adzes, knives for reaping the harvest and implements for grinding corn, were found.

Canaanite war-chariots galloping to battle. Reconstruction of ivory plaque from Megiddo.

The dependence of the farmer on natural phenomena caused the creation of a new cult — the cult of fertility. This cult was to remain one of the most important cults in subsequent ages. In the Pottery-Neolithic culture it is represented by a large number of stone and clay figurines of the Mother-Goddess, sometimes portrayed naturalistically, and sometimes in the form of a schematic representation of the female reproductive organs.

THE CHALCOLITHIC PERIOD.   This period began at about 4,000 BC. Stone was still much used for making tools and weapons, but the first metal used by men, copper, made its appearance at this time, and hence derived the name of this period.

The Egyptian war against the inhabitants of the Syro-Palestinian region, depicted on a panel on the exterior of the chariot of Pharaoh Thutmosis IV, giving a detailed picture of the armor used in warfare. End of the 15th century BC.

Until not very long ago it was thought that copper occurred only sporadically, and that it was used sparingly for special purposes only. This assumption was challenged with the discovery of a treasure of copper vessels in a cave — the Cave of the Treasure — in the region of the Dead Sea. We shall probably never know the identity of the people who concealed their most precious belongings in the cave, nor what calamity forced them to do so, and prevented their coming back to recover it. Nevertheless, it showed how faulty were previous appraisals of the period.

The people who concealed this treasure were excellent farmers. This is indicated by the remains of wheat and barley, lentils, onions and garlic found in the same cave. There were also elaborate pottery vessels, grinding-bowls made of stone, wickerwork baskets and sieves, textiles and an upright loom on which these had been woven. Among the remains of animals found in the cave were the bones of sheep, goats, deer, gazelles, and fowl.

These were but a prelude to the most tantalizing find — 429 vessels of copper. About one half of the find consisted of mace-heads of various sizes, attesting to a warrior nation. Then came four score of rods, some hollow, others solid, decorated with engravings and figurines of birds, animals, and human faces. There also were ten "crowns", too small and too heavy to be worn by a normal human head. Finally, there was a score of axes and chisels, employed in the making of these implements. An uncompleted mace-head indicates that the technique of casting known as 'vanishing wax' was known to these early

Color fresco-fragments from Tuleilat Ghassul on the bank of the River Jordan, dating to the Prehistoric (Chalcolithic) period, reflecting, perhaps, an ancient ritual myth. The motif of an eight horned star is repeated several times.

coppersmiths. Not far from this cave, at the oasis of Engeddi, was discovered a large temple of this period, from which some of these obscure artefacts might have come.

GHASSUL AND BEERSHEBA.　　The Chalcolithic culture was basically one of shepherds and farmers, and it is for this reason that the major sites pertaining to this period were located in the larger valleys of the Holy Land, such as the Jordan Valley and along the coastal plain.

Our first acquaintance with a Chalcolithic site in the Holy Land was made some 40 years ago in the lower Jordan Valley, at several small mounds known by the name of Tuleilat el-Ghassul, northeast of Jericho. On one of these mounds a fairly large Chalcolithic settlement was discovered.

Narrow alleys and small public squares separated the simple houses from each other. These were oblong mud-brick structures, consisting each of a larger hall behind which was a smaller chamber. Within the dwellings and all around them were a large number of storage pits in which grain was kept. The walls of some of these houses were plastered and beautifully painted in bright colors. In one house there was depicted some kind of procession. In another there was a large 'star' and several large 'eyes'. The quality of these early paintings is not inferior to that of the copper implements.

Copper was very rare at Ghassul; implements were mainly of stone. However, there was some improvement in the production of pottery. The larger vessels were still hand-made, on a mat, as is indicated by the impressions left by the mat on the bases of the vessels. But the introduction of a slow turning potter's wheel permitted the production of smaller vessels, such as jugs, cups and drinking-horns. A very interesting vessel was the one the excavators, for lack of a better term, named the 'bird-shaped vessel'. This was later recognized as a churn, in which milk was shaken into cheese and butter.

THE BEERSHEBA CHALCOLITHIC CULTURE.　　Some 25 years ago several small mounds were discovered on the northern bank of Nahal Beersheba, the dry wadi forming the border between the sown land to the north and Negev desert to the south. These sites were occupied during the second half of the 4th millenium BC.

The houses of these settlers were subterranean, excavated in the soft loess. Each house consisted of subterranean rooms connected by underground tunnels. Cooking was done in a sunken open-air court, which also provided ventilation and lighting.

The inhabitants of these settlements were occupied mainly in farming, and the husbandry of sheep and goats. Some, however, smelted copper brought to this place from mines in the *Arabah* to the southeast. Others made beautiful three-legged bowls of basalt brought from the same location where the copper was mined. As is attested by various materials, these settlers were also very actively occupied in international trade. There were also several artists who made exquisite carvings in ivory (elephant tusks were also found in the Cave of the Treasure).

At some of the sites at Beer Safad were found ivory figurines representing human beings in a rigid posture, as well as heads of animals and birds. Sometimes the forehead, the sides of the head and the cheeks were perforated, for the insertion of hair; the eyes were sunk, and inlaid by some paste or shell. Jewelery was also produced in profusion, and consisted mainly of small pendants of bone, ivory, limestone, slate or turquoise. Among the imported materials found at Beersheba there were also mother of pearl and carnelian, both employed in the making of jewelery. Some products were found at this site, others only at another, so that there seems to have been some kind of specialization. This applies also to the production of copper, from which mace-heads, axes, chisels, points of awls and various ornaments were made. All were cast in the technique of 'vanishing wax'. Indeed, fireplaces with dross, stone anvils for the breaking up of ore, and smelting tools were found at some of the Beersheba sites.

The sophistication of the various aspects of life, so well expressed in the local art, also finds expression in the attitude of the Chalcolithic societies of the Holy Land toward the dead. Infants were interred below the floors of houses, a practice which was to increase in the subsequent Bronze Age. Adults were brought to burial in a temporary grave, from which the bones were taken after some time and placed in large leather bags. These were then buried in unused corn-pits, to ensure that the soul of the dead man would live on in the family.

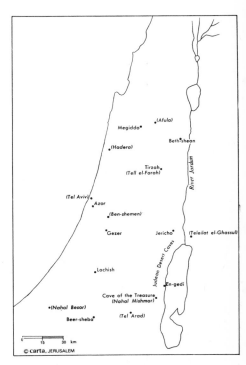

The Chalcolithic period.
4th millennium BC.

THE NORTHERN CHALCOLITHIC CULTURE.

In contrast to the rather simple burial customs of the Beersheba settlers, the northern Chalcolithic communities developed a much more sophisticated culture. In the cemeteries discovered at Azor near Tel Aviv, Bene Beraq, Hederah, and in some other places in the north of the Holy Land, clay ossuaries were discovered. These were sometimes made in the form of a jar, but more common were ossuaries in the form of a house or a shrine, of a gabled façade, with a window below the gable, for the insertion of loose bones. Sometimes palm branches adorned these small mortuary shrines. At Azor, the largest of the Chalcolithic necropoli in the Holy Land, some 120 ossuaries were found. Miniature ossuaries were sometimes placed as an offering within larger ones.

The Assyrian attack on the city of Eqron in Philistia depicted on a relief from the palace of Sargon. 6th century AD.

THE HISTORIC PERIOD; THE BRONZE AGE.

Various materials and artifacts discovered at sites in the Holy Land relating to the Chalcolithic period attest to the fact that commercial relations were established with foreign countries as early as the 4th millenium BC. But it was only in the Bronze Age that firm commercial and cultural relations were established between the Holy Land and the neighboring empires, first with Mesopotamia, and later also with Egypt.

For about 2,000 years — in the 3rd and 2nd millenia BC — bronze was the chief material employed in the production of tools, weapons and jewelery, hence the name of this archaeological period. Some scholars, however, prefer the term 'Canaanite' for this age, naming it after the most important culture in the region extending from the borders of Asia Minor to the north as far as the Red Sea to the south.

INTERNAL ORGANIZATION.

The Holy Land, which had by now become a flourishing country, rich in corn, olive oil, herds of cattle and flocks of sheep and goats, exporting its products north and south, was a worthwhile target for the neighboring empires, mainly Egypt. The constant menace of its neighbors compelled the local rulers to construct strong defenses in various parts of the country. Such undertakings could by no means be accomplished by a single village. It was in this way that the whole country came to be divided into a large number of small city states, at the center of each of which stood the king of the city and his entourage, trading protection for the fruits of the land. The city was always located on some high ground, in the vicinity of a copious spring. It was always fortified by a massive wall, behind which the farmers of the surrounding villages could find shelter in cases of emergency. On the higher part of the hill were erected the king's palace and the temple. Throughout the Bronze Age mud-brick was the chief construction material, of which walls, gates, palaces, temples and dwellings were made. These were quite frequently destroyed, and had to be rebuilt from time to time. It is for this reason that sites occupied during the Bronze Age produced the typical mound, known in this part of the world by the name of *tel*.

THE EARLY BRONZE AGE

This period, beginning at the end of the 3rd millenium BC, lasted for about 1,000 years. It is at this time that a large number of cities were founded, many of which were to become prominent in the biblical narrative. Among these were Ai, Megiddo, Beth Shean, Jericho, Lachish and Arad.

The Early Bronze Age is the beginning of the historical period for the two most important cultures in the ancient Near East, Egypt and Mesopotamia. Although no inscriptions of the 3rd millenium BC have as yet been found in the Holy Land, those found in the neighboring countries shed light on the situation in the Holy Land as well. One relief found in a 25th century BC tomb in Egypt depicts the conquest of a fortified city, which is thought to be in the land of Canaan, and the names adjoining it seem to be Semitic. One century later dates the description of the military campaign by Veni, an Egyptian general, against the 'Amu', the name of the inhabitants of the Holy Land at that time. These frequent military campaigns attest to troublesome times in Egypt, when the Old Empire was coming to an end. This loosening of the Egyptian grip brought the Holy Land into closer contact with the empire of Mesopotamia. During the 24th century BC the separate city states of southern Mesopotamia unified into the Sumerain kingdom. In the same century this was replaced by the Semitic-Accadian kingdom under the leadership of Sargon. This enormous kingdom embraced all the countries between the Tigris and the Euphrates. The heirs of Sargon extended his kingdom by the conquest of the land of Amuru, the biblical Amorites, to the west and even reached Egypt. At about 2180 BC this kingdom, too, came to an end, marking the end of the Early Bronze Age in Mesopotamia. Because of the

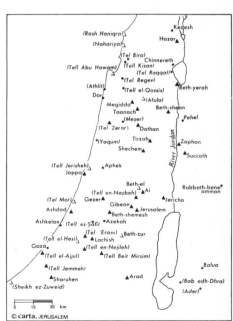

The Canaanite period.
3150–1200 BC.

thick accumulation of debris of the cities — in some cases a city was destroyed and rebuilt not less than 25 times — only limited sections of Early Bronze occupation levels have as yet been excavated. Thus, we know very little of their urban planning. However, what we do know is that all of these cities were provided with formidable systems of fortification, and that in most of them there were public buildings of great size. Thus, at Ai, apart from a series of extremely strong walls, there was also discovered a fortified palace (some, however, prefer to identify it as a temple); at Beth Yerah, a huge mound situated southwest of the Sea of Galilee, one of the most fertile regions in the country, both a formidable system of fortifications and part of a very large building identified as a granary have been unearthed. At Megiddo, too, the city was strongly fortified. Not far from the city walls a shrine was constructed consisting of an eliptic high-place of 10 m diameter. As was the case at other sites, all the shrines and temples constructed at Megiddo over a 2,000 year period were located in the vicinity of this ancient site.

During the Early Bronze Age there is noted a phenomenon which was to be felt even more strongly in the subsequent period. The Holy Land, small as it is, has always been exposed to influences from different directions. Thus, there is a marked difference in shape, production techniques and decoration of the pottery of various regions of the country. It is only by the analysis of the various ceramic groups produced in the different regions throughout the 3rd millenium BC that a division of this 1,000 year long period may be subdivided into four cultural and chronological phases. Thus, red burnished bowls were typical of the southern part of the country, whereas in the north there were families of gray, red and black burnished vessels contemporary with the southern types. The same would apply to the preference for certain shapes in this or that region of the country.

THE MIDDLE BRONZE AGE

The decline of the 1,000 years of the Early Bronze Age is marked by a destruction of the flourishing city states, caused by an invasion of the new peoples who penetrated the Holy Land from the north and east. Some of these invaders were Semites, the fathers of the Hebrews. The exact date of the Age of the Patriarchs is not known. Some scholars would place it in the 21st–19th centuries BC, while others prefer a later date in the Hyksos period, in the 18–16th centuries BC. Although the wanderings of Abraham, Isaac and Jacob were connected with sites which were to become prominent in the later history of the Holy Land, it is extremely difficult to find archaeological evidence for these events. This period, the 21st–19th centuries BC, is sometimes named the Age of the Patriarchs. A little later, during the 19th–18 centuries BC, pressure from the West Semites caused the fall of the Sumerian and Accadian kingdoms, paving the way for the Old Kingdom of Babylon, the most famous ruler of which was Hamurabi (1728–1688 BC), the lawgiver, whose laws greatly influenced the code of laws of the Hebrews. This kingdom mastered one of the most imporant international trade routes, the King's Highway, running from Mesopotamia and Syria to the Gulf of Elath. It is via one of the branches of this road, running west to the Holy Land, that Jacob went to the land of Canaan (*Genesis: 31–34*). By using other branches of the same road the Patriarchs made their journey to Egypt.

To the period just preceding the rule of Hamurabi belong some 35,000 clay tablets found at Mari, a large city of Syria, on the Euphrates. These were documents written in the Accadian cuneiform script, containing diplomatic letters, dealing with matters of the management of the state, law and economy. Some of the letters dealt with the internal affairs of the kingdom of Mari, while

A group of men and women of a West Semitic tribe, going down to Egypt. An Egyptian wall painting from the latter part of the 19th century BC, found at the tomb of Beni Hasan (Egypt).

others were copies of letters sent to rulers of other countries. It is in these letters that the *Habiru* are mentioned, referring possibly to the Hebrews. It seems that the tribe of Benjamin is mentioned in these letters as well.

THE HOLY LAND IN THE MIDDLE BRONZE AGE.   From the other side of the ancient Near East, from Egypt, come other documents referring to the Holy Land. One of these is the Sinuhe Scroll which refers to Egyptian rule over the Holy Land. Another interesting piece of evidence is a painting found in a tomb at Bani Hasan in Egypt, showing a caravan of merchants conveying kohl from the country to the east of the Jordan to Egypt.

Of more importance still are the two groups of documents known as the Excecration Text. The two groups belong to the 20th and 19th centuries BC respectively. In these documents are cursed rulers of various cities, enemies of the Egyptian Pharaohs. Many of these cities are in the Holy Land—Jerusalem, Askelon, Aphek, Accho, Beth Shean, Laish (Dan of later times), Hazor and a large number of others. These texts attest to the continuous attempt made by the Egyptians to conquer the land of Canaan. These attempts came to an abrupt end, however, by the end of the 18th century BC, when the strong Middle Empire was shattered by the Hyksos, who were referred to in Egyptian documents as "rulers of foreign countries". To this period belongs the earliest inscription found in the Holy Land, written in the obscure Semitic script known as Proto-Canaanite.

During the 18th and 17th centuries BC Egypt itself had been conquered by the western Semitic tribes, known as the Hyksos, who ruled during these centuries over the whole of Syria and the Holy Land as well.

After a period of unrest the local city states emerged anew and began to rebuild their defenses. The Hyksos rulers had introduced the horse into the warfare of the Middle East for speed, and the horse-drawn war-chariot, and the battering-ram. These in turn caused a revolutionary change in the methods of fortification. In order to make the approach to the foot of the walls more difficult the slopes of the mounds were smoothed down at a gradient of 45°. The whole slope was then covered by layers of crushed stone, bricks, pounded earth, stones and their like, in order to form a slippery surface, difficult of ascent. Sometimes a dry moat was added at the foot of the slope, making the approach of chariots still more difficult. The wall itself was erected at the top of the slope. A similar change was also introduced in the planning of the gate, the most vulnerable point in the city's defenses. Whereas in the earlier period the gate allowed only indirect entry, which means that the entrant had to make a right turn on entering the gate, exposing his right arm to the defenders. The new gates, which had to admit chariots as well, were now of a direct approach type. In order to remedy this drawback of direct approach, the gates were now made much deeper, by the addition of several bays, one behind the other. Equally, the approach to the gate itself was changed; instead of the steps which led to the gate in the Early Bronze Age, a ramp was now made in order to facilitate the ascent of a horse-drawn chariot.

The weapons of this period were all made of bronze. The simple maces of earlier times were now replaced by lances, spears, swords and cutting axes, and the arch, a long range weapon, had also been introduced.

At several sites in the Holy Land private dwellings have been unearthed. These consisted of a rather large court around which were arranged rooms on one, two, three or four sides of the court, depending on the wealth of the owner. In the court there were a cistern, storage bins, cooking and baking ovens. In the better houses the rooms on the ground floor housed the stables, cowsheds and workshops, while the lodgings were on the upper floor.

CULT LIFE.   There was a marked elaboration in both temple building and the religious ritual of this period. At Megiddo the high-place was rebuilt and nearby three new temples were erected, each dedicated to a different deity. The temples were now built according to a new scheme — a tripartite plan, in which a porch supported by two columns led into a hall, behind which was the Holy of Holies. This became the basic plan of all Canaanite temples, and was later adopted by the builders of the Temple of Solomon in Jerusalem. In the Holy Land temples on this plan were found mostly in the larger cities, such as Hazor and Megiddo, on the Mediterranean coast, north of Acre.

Unique in its form was the high-place discovered at Middle Bronze Age Gezer. It consisted of a row of ten upright monoliths — *massebot* of the Bible — placed in the center of the mound.

Baal the Canaanite deity, often mentioned in the Bible, depicted on a limestone stele from Ugarith, holding a thunderbolt in his left hand and a baton in his right. 14th century BC.

Detail of painted Philistine pottery sherds from Megiddo depicting a harp-player with animals listening.

POTTERY. The pottery of this period, all made on the potter's wheel, attained perfection both in delicacy of ware, grace of form and the quality of decoration. The potters of the Hyksos period have produced an easily recognizable juglet, piriform in shape, decorated by geometric patterns, made by a fine pointed tool, filled-in with a white substance. In the performance of certain cults was employed a small bowl to the base of which were attached seven small cups, each for a different ingredient. Imports from Mediterranean countries abound in the Middle Bronze Age.

BURIAL. The belief in an after-life seems to have been more widespread at this period. For this reason most tombs were filled with numerous pottery vessels in which food and drink were supplied. It is also common to find weapons with the men and jewelery with the women, who were also supplied with cosmetic implements. In some cases a warrior would be placed in his tomb together with his horse.

THE LATE BRONZE AGE

In the middle of the 16th century BC the 350 year long rule of the Hyksos ended. The rulers of the New Empire of Egypt embarked on the conquest of the land of Canaan. The greatest of them, Thutmosis III (1469–1436 BC) defeated a coalition of the kings of Syria and the Holy Land. In his geographical lists he mentions 118 fortified cities which he conquered in the land of Canaan alone.

The political and social situation in the Holy Land during the Late Bronze Age is well reflected in the royal archives of Amenophis III (1413–1377 BC) and of Akhenaten (1377–1360 BC). These consist of a large number of letters found at El Amarna in Egypt, written in the Accadian cuneiform script, which by this time had become the international language used in diplomatic dealings and commercial transactions. In it were written also religio-literary writings. From these letters, many of which were sent to, or received from, rulers in the land of Canaan, we learn that the country was inhabited by a mixed stock of West Semites, Hurians (the Horites of the Bible, cf. *Genesis 14:6; 36:2,* etc.) and other peoples. The Canaanites (this name occurs frequently in contemporary literature) spoke the Canaanite language, the language of the West Semites, although in writing the Accadian cuneiform script was much employed. Accadian was a syllabic script. More advanced, and quite frequently employed was the ugaritic alphabetic script, named after Ugarit in Syria, where it was discovered. It, too, was a cuneiform script, but the number of letters was 31 only. This language belonged to the Semitic family of languages. Closest to the later Hebrew language was Canaanite, i.e., the language spoken by the inhabitants of the land of Canaan.

Although various cities worshipped various gods, they all belonged to the Canaanite pantheon, best known from Ugaritic literature. El and Ashera were the genitors of the gods. The king of the gods was Baal, the Lord, many cities possessing their own Baal. Apart from these, there were a large number of lesser deities. Frequently gods were interchanged or assimilated. Thus, Ashera was identified with Anat and Ashtoret. All of these gods are mentioned in the Bible. The Canaanite religious cults were infested with sexual promiscuity, male and female prostitutes were regularly employed in the service of the Canaanite temples. Human sacrifices were common, and very popular was the cult of snakes. We learn of all of this not only from Canaanite literature, but also from the many references to the heathen ways of the Canaanites in the Bible.

The determining factor in the history and archaeology of the Holy Land in the Late Bronze Age was the rise of the great empires of Babylon to the east and Egypt to the south, where the New Kingdom replaced the Hyksos rulers. Most of Syria and the Holy Land were under Egyptian domination. The internal division of the country into a large number of city states, each ruled by its own ruler (the biblical 'kings' of Canaan) still prevailed. At certain places in the country, such as at Beth Shean in the north, Egyptian garrisons were posted, which kept close watch over the local rulers. Throughout most of this period the country thrived and was truly a land of milk and honey.

A Philistine warship (model).
c. 1200 BC.

FORTIFICATIONS. The strong fortifications constructed in the preceding period were still in use throughout the Late Bronze Age: only repairs were needed here and there. The dry moats and the sloping taluses were for the most part abandoned (at Lachish, for instance, temples were built where once there had been a moat). In some of the cities a citadel was built within the walls in order to accomodate the Egyptian garrison, as was the case at Beth Shean, and in most cases a fortified palace was built in the near vicinity of the gate.

TEMPLES. The Late Bronze Age temples followed the plan laid down in the Middle Bronze Age (there was no ethnic change in the Holy Land). The number of temples greatly increased, and in some of the cities there were three or more shrines, each probably dedicated to a different deity. In some of these temples as, for example, at Hazor, there were found statues of the deities still in their shrines with the offerings, brought in bowls, still in place. The deities venerated in these temples belonged to the Canaanite pantheon, many of which are known from the biblical narrative and contemporary Canaanite literature.

THE DEVELOPMENT OF WRITING. The development of writing began in the 4th millenium BC both in Mesopotamia and in Egypt. In the latter every idea was expressed at the beginning by a picture, named pictograph. At the next stage of development the pictures underwent a process of abstraction, each picture representing a syllable. The system never reached the stage of an alphabetic script. The development of writing in Mesopotamia originally followed the same line of development. Here, too, pictographs were employed in the early stages. But as the writing material mostly employed was clay (in contrast to the stone and papyrus in Egypt) on which the symbols were marked by a stylus, the syllables which replaced the pictographs took the form of wedges of triangular heads or tails. The transition from the syllabic cuneiform script into the Canaanite alphabetic script is still obscure. During the 2nd millenium BC there were several scripts current in the Holy Land, each represented by an extremely small number of inscriptions. The best-known of these is the so called proto-Sinaitic script, several inscriptions of which were discovered in the Egyptian turquoise mines in Sinai, where Semitic slaves were employed. Some of the 40 extant symbols of this script bear great resemblance to the Canaanite scripts current in the Holy Land. There are still many links missing in the chain linking this script to the much later Hebrew alphabet.

Although writing in religious life and diplomatic intercourse became a very common phenomenon in the Late Bronze Age, written documents originating in the Holy Land are still scarce. One of the few extant documents is a fragment of the Gilgamesh epic, which was found by a shepherd on the slope of the mound of Megiddo. It is written in Accadian, the international language of the age. From Beth Shean comes a stele written in the Egyptian hieroglyphic script, and most recently a dictionary of the Accadian and the more ancient Sumerian languages has been found at Tel Aphek in the Sharon.

This alphabetical script known as "Proto-Sinaitic", inscribed on an Egyptian sandstone statuette was, perhaps, made by Semitic miners employed by the Egyptians in the copper mines of Sinai. Dating from the 14th century BC, it is the earliest found alphabetical script, the prototype of the Phoenician script in which the Hebrew script originated. The inscription reads: "For the Lady (goddess)", and was found at the temple of Serabit el-Khadem, Sinai.

CULTURAL RELATIONS AND POTTERY.   During the Late Bronze Age the Holy Land was not only a bridge by means of which cultural exchange occurred between the great empires; it also developed closer relations with the Mediterranean world. These cultural connections were already established by the later phases of the Middle Bronze Age. Thus, pottery was being imported from Cyprus by that time, though commercial relations developed on a much greater scale only in the Late Bronze Age. In addition to Cypriote pottery, ceramics were also imported from Crete and Mycenae on the Greek mainland. (In many cases the pottery found in the Holy Land was simply a container in which certain substances were imported from abroad). Many of these foreign wares were imitated by local potters.

In the Holy Land itself there sprang up a ceramic industry the products of which were not inferior to imported wares. One of the larger potters' workshops was located at Tell el-Ajjul (identified with Beth Eglaim) in the south of the country. Its products are known by the name of Bichrome ware. Bowls and jugs produced by these potters were decorated with geometric patterns, birds and animals painted in red and black.

BURIAL.   The economic and cultural prosperity of the Holy Land in the Late Bronze Age is also well reflected in the rich finds in the tombs of this period. Extremely rich were the finds in the necropoli of Megiddo, Jericho, Lachish, Tell el-Ajjul, etc. The tombs of richer people were filled almost to the brim with pottery which contained foodstuffs and drinks of all kinds, furniture and jewelery.

IVORIES.   The wealth of the local Canaanite rulers may also be judged by the treasury of the kings of Megiddo. A 'strong-room' was discovered in the palace close-by the city gate. These treasures were collected over a period of hundreds of years and almost took the form of a museum by the beginning of the Iron Age, the date of the latest acquisition, the earliest dating to the Middle Bronze Age. Among the treasures were gold vessels, lapis lazuli, and an extremely large number of carved ivories, some of which are of the Middle Bronze Age, but for the most part they are of the Late Bronze. The latest pieces were of the Iron Age, a time when Megiddo was still ruled by the Canaanites.

Stele of Mesha, king of Moab, c. 850 BC. The inscription in Moabite dialect is written in ancient Hebrew Script, and describes the king's wars against Israel.

The borders of the tribal territories.
12th to 11th century BC.

THE IRON AGE

ISRAELITES AND PHILISTINES.   During the latter part of the 13th century BC there began an infiltration into the Holy Land of Israelite tribes from the east and of the Sea Peoples from the west and south. This infiltration was preceded in the later decades of the Late Bronze Age by a slackening of Egypt's grip over the Holy Land, followed by internal strife between the local kings, each of whom attempted to enlarge his territory. This prolonged period of struggle and unrest greatly weakened the Canaanite city states and paved the way for the Philistines, who were part of the movement of the Sea Peoples and of the Israelites.

Israelite tribes crossed the Jordan under the leadership of Joshua and began the conquest of those parts of the land of Canaan which were not thickly populated, mainly the mountainous regions of Judah and Ephraim. The conquest of the relatively strong Canaanite cities was a prolonged process which lasted about two centuries.

Archaeological remains left behind by the Israelite tribes in these early centuries are both scant and poor, consisting mostly of rather poor, coarse pottery, and dull structures. In many cases the arrival of the Israelites in the Holy Land may best be studied in their destruction of many of the Late Bronze cities. It was only after the establishment of the kingdoms of Saul, David and Solomon that we find again fortified citadels and cities, replacing the Canaanite city states, or walled-in places which were not settled before.

The Philistines, on the other hand, are easily recognizable from the moment of their arrival in the Holy Land. The new and vigorous maritime tribes arrived in this part of the world from the Aegean islands, crossing the Balkans and Asia Minor on their way. They brought with them the secret of casting and of forging iron, from which their weapons and tools were made. These were much more efficient than the ones made of bronze, possessed by the Egyptians and Canaanites. Combining the efficiency of the iron weapons with that of the light horse-drawn chariot, the Philistines swept the country, conquered the whole of the Mediterranean coastal plain (the Land of the Philistines of the Bible), penetrated deep into the mountainous areas, subduing Israelite tribes, and even penetrated into the Valley of Jezreel as far as Beth Shean.

PHILISTINE POTTERY AND BURIAL CUSTOMS. The presence of the Philistines in the Holy Land is best attested by their ceramic art and their burial customs. The Philistines produced pottery which originated in Mycenae, but it is certainly not free of Egyptian and local Canaanite influences. Their vessels, mostly jugs and craters, were painted in black and red. The decoration is frequently in geometric patterns, but men, animals and birds, especially these latter, are also frequent.

Large Philistine cemeteries were discovered at Tel Sharuhen (Tell el Far'a) in the south of the country and at Beth Shean in the north. Typical of these burials are large clay coffins shaped in the form of a man. The origin of this burial custom is not yet fully understood, but it is thought that the Philistines copied this practice from the Egyptian nobility, which had resorted to it in the Late Bronze Age. A 14th–13th century BC necropolis was recently discovered at Deir el-Balaḥ, on the border between the Holy Land and Egypt.

THE ISRAELITE CITIES. The Israelite kingdom was created by Saul and David. After the establishment of his kingship at Hebron, David set out in 1010 BC to conquer the stronghold of Zion, seat of the Jebusite ruler, naming it the City of David, and capital of his kingdom. But it was left to Solomon to build Jerusalem and the Temple, and to establish royal power throughout the country. The whole of the country was divided into 12 administrative units, and at strategic points royal cities were founded. Three of these cities have been excavated — Hazor in the Galilee, Megiddo in the Valley of Jezreel, and Gezer in the coastal plain. They were all planned and fortified by the royal authorities. This is conspicuous in the planning of the walls and the city gates, which are all of the same plan and of about the same measurements. There were royal storehouses such as the one discovered in the vicinity of the Gate at Hazor. These cities housed the horses and the chariots of the king's army, like the ones

Illustration of the probable appearance of Lachish, before its destruction by the Assyrians, depicting the city's double-wall fortications, built by king Rehoboam, the palace-fort in the center with towers and buildings.

discovered at Megiddo. The united Israelite kingdom extended from Dan in the north to Beersheba in the south, at both of which archaeological research is now in progress. On the borders of the kingdom royal fortresses were constructed. One of these has been unearthed at Arad, on the border between Judah and the Negev.

THE ISRAELITE HOUSEHOLD.   Throughout the whole of the Bronze Age the courtyard type of house was the most common private dwelling. A change in the design of the house was introduced during the Israelite period. In archaeological literature this type of house is known as the Four Space House, and has regularly been a two-storey house, built of mud-brick on a foundation of field-stones. It consisted of an oblong court, partly covered and partly open-air, along three sides of which there were rooms, at least one of which was always open to the court. In the court there was generally a cistern, ovens for baking and cooking, and storage-bins. The rooms on the lower floor contained workshops, the kitchen and the dining room. The biblical "table" was in fact a round mat or skin placed on the ground, on which food was served.

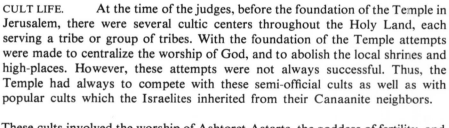

A panel from the 'Black obelisk' of Shalmanezer III, depicting Jehu, king of Israel, bowing in submission, before the Assyrian king, while behind him are Assyrian guards and Israelite escorts bearing tribute.

CULT LIFE.   At the time of the judges, before the foundation of the Temple in Jerusalem, there were several cultic centers throughout the Holy Land, each serving a tribe or group of tribes. With the foundation of the Temple attempts were made to centralize the worship of God, and to abolish the local shrines and high-places. However, these attempts were not always successful. Thus, the Temple had always to compete with these semi-official cults as well as with popular cults which the Israelites inherited from their Canaanite neighbors.

These cults involved the worship of Ashtoret-Astarte, the goddess of fertility, and the burning of incense. The semi-official cult shrines were mostly located in far-away places, such as Dan in the north, or in the recently discovered southern sites at Arad and Beersheba, the horned altar of which has been preserved.

THE HEBREW SCRIPT AND INSCRIPTIONS.   The Hebrews adopted the Canaanite alphabetic script sometime in the 12th or 11th century BC, developing from it their own specific script. The earliest Hebrew document written in this script is a limestone tablet found at Gezer, known as the Gezer Calendar. This is followed by the commercial documents written on potsherds found at Shomron, the capital of the rival kingdom of Israel. Another large and important Hebrew document is the inscription engraved at the outlet of the Siloam Tunnel. The latest Judean documents are the letters found at Lachish, which vividly portray the state of affairs in Judah on the eve of the destruction of the First Temple. Apart from official documents there have also been found an exceedingly large number of seals, some of government officials, but mostly of private people. To the first class belongs the seal of Shema, Servant of Jeroboam, found at Megiddo, or that of Jaazaniahu, Servant of the King, found at Tell en-Naṣbeh, identified with biblical Mizpah, north of Jerusalem.

Forming a class on their own are the numerous stamped jar handles on which occur the four names Hebron, Ziph, Socho and *mmsht,* the first three being most probably the names of the royal administrative centers in which taxes paid in kind were collected, the fourth possibly meaning "the government". The jars stamps signified that the contents of the jars had been verified by the tax authorities.

WATER SUPPLY.   Towns and villages were regularly established in the vicinity of springs. In areas where the supply of the spring was insufficient, or in order to avoid going daily to the source, cisterns were excavated in many houses in the rock. However, in the larger cities, the authorities wishing to ensure a constant supply of water even in cases of emergency, brought the water from a spring into the city by means of a tunnel excavated in the rock; the water was then drawn by means of a shaft many meters deep. Such large-scale engineering undertakings were discovered at Megiddo, Hazor, Gezer (the Gezer tunnel was excavated in the Late Bronze Age), Lachish and Jerusalem. In the last mentioned city there were several attempts to bring the water of the Gihon spring into the city, the most successful one being that of King Hezekiah.

THE ECONOMY.   Judah and Israel were basically agricultural states, producing mainly wheat, barley, olive oil and wine. For this we have the evidence of the Bible, as well as that of hundreds of wine- and olive-presses found all over the country. Much of the oil was exported to the neighboring countries, whence timber and items of luxury were imported in return. Some of the imports came from as far as south Arabia. The active internal commercial activities involved the introduction of an official system of weights and measures. Indeed, hundreds of stone weights of various values, like neṣef, pym and beqa, have been found at Israelite sites.

Girl with timbrel, found at Shikmona excavations. Israelite period.

THE ARTS. The local artistic products of the country, as may be seen mostly in the pottery, are basically those of a land of farmers and small artisans. The pottery is simple, of nicely made and graceful shapes, but far from the luxurious products of the richer neighboring countries. No statuary or reliefs of stone are extant, possibly because of religious inhibitions. It is for this reason that the richer classes of citizens and royalty depended on imported art objects. To this class would thus belong the ivories found in the palaces of the Israelite kings at Shomron, Megiddo, Lachish and Hazor. These ivory carvings reflect the contemporary art of the ancient Near East, much better known from Assyrian palaces and from northern Syria, in which Phoenician and Egyptian artistic elements mingled.

ON PROPHECY. Although Israelite prophecy is perhaps the best-known, it was by no means limited to them alone. Prophets conveying the wish of the gods were known at Mari, as is attested by ten documents found in the archives there. These, and some of the biblical prophecies, were obtained by dreams. Prophecy was also known to a certain extent in Phoenicia and Aram, as well as in Babylonia, from which Balaam originated. The main difference between the prophecy of Israel and that of other contemporary nations lies in the moral message which the Israelite prophets conveyed, contrary to the practical purposes of the prophecy of the others. Prophecy was closely connected with witchcraft and divination. For this certain aids were needed, some of which were criticised in the Bible. One of these aids was the entrails of sacrificial animals, mainly the liver. Two clay livers with magical formulae inscribed on them were found in the Holy Land.

THE PERSIAN PERIOD

In 586 BC the Babylonians destroyed the Temple of Jerusalem and deported a large part of the population, destroying numerous other towns and villages. The recovery was a very slow process. When Cyrus ascended the throne of the Persian empire the Jews were allowed to return to their homeland and a new era began.

The archaeological finds of this period are rather poor. There were larger buildings discovered on those sites which housed palaces of local governors of the Persian satrapy, located at strategic points, such as Hazor, Megiddo and

Lachish. Otherwise the finds of this period are rather dull, consisting mostly of pottery, coins struck by the local Jewish authorities, and seal impressions on jar handles, on which is the name of the province, Yahud, the city of Jerusalem or the name of the ruling official, all inscribed in Aramaic, which became the current language and script, replacing Hebrew. During this period relations between the Holy Land and the Greek islands and mainland strengthened, as is evinced by numerous Greek coins and Greek pottery of the 6th–4th centuries BC found in large quantities all over the country.

The division of the Kingdom into Judah and Israel. 928 BC.

THE HELLENISTIC PERIOD

The conquest of the whole of the east by Alexander the Great brought the Holy Land closer than ever to the orbit of the Western world. At the beginning of this era the Holy Land was divided into several political-ethnic units: Judea formed rather a small territory culturally and religiously independent. To the north of Judea lay the larger Samaritan distrinct, inhabited by descendants of peoples who were brought to that region by the Assyrians after the subjugation of the Israelite kingdom. These peoples were later known by the name of Samaritans, after the district in which they were settled. Enmity reigned between the Samaritans and the returning Jews. The coast and the coastal plain were inhabited by a mixed population, but since the Persian period the dominating ethnic element in this region were Phoenicians, who established maritime colonies along the coast, penetrating as far east as Marisa in Idumaea. The southern part of the Judean mountains was populated by Edomites who migrated there on the eve of the Persian period.

The policy of Alexander the Great and his Ptolemaic and Seleucid heirs was to implant Greek colonies wherever possible, in order to serve as centers for the diffusion of Greek culture. The most famous colonies in the Holy Land were those of Acre-Accho-Ptolemais on the coast, and Samaria inland. The slackening of Seleucid rule by the middle of the 2nd century BC encouraged the Jews, among other peoples, to fight for independence. Rebellion began with the revolt of the Jews under the leadership of the Maccabean family and culminated in the foundation of a Judean state under the rule of the Hasmonean dynasty. At the end of Alexander Jannaeus' reign the Hasmonean kingdom extended over the whole of the country to the west of the Jordan, as far as the territory of Acre in the north to Gaza in the south. It also included the Jewish region of the Peraea to the east of the Jordan, the Golan and Bashan in the north, and parts of Moab in the south of the country east of the Jordan. The Hasmonean kings embarked on a plan to convert to Judaism the foreign peoples dwelling to the west of the Jordan, and in this way the Idumeans became part of the Jewish state.

This was the state of affairs in the Holy Land until 63 BC, when the whole of the east came under the Roman yoke. The independence of the Jewish state was retained, but the coastal cities were granted autonomy and were governed directly by the authorities of the Roman province of Syria. This arrangement was to become a source of trouble in the following centuries.

Culturally the Holy Land became part of the Hellenized world. Althought the number of sites of the Hellenistic period which have been investigated is small, there is enough evidence to show that Greek classical architectural orders were employed in the Holy Land in this period. The local pottery was predominantly influenced by Hellenistic types and imports abound. Even the autonomous Jewish coins, struck by the Hasmorean rulers in Jerusalem, bear resemblance to contemporary Hellenistic issues, although they avoided the use of objects alien to Jewish religious feelings.

A silver coin struck at Acre *c.* 310 BC, depicting Alexander the Great of Macedon.

The Hellenistic-western influence was decisive in all other aspects of material and cultural life. Greek became the main language of the inscriptions of all ethnic groups (Aramaic reemerged again only in the Roman period), and only few pottery types are sufficiently free of Hellenistic influence to be considered purely local.

THE ROMAN PERIOD

Politically, but certainly not culturally, the Holy Land became part of the Roman orbit in 63 BC, when the country was conquered by Pompey. The current chronology tends to begin the Roman period in the Holy Land in 37 BC, with the ascendance of Herod the Great to the throne. This is more satisfactory than the previous date, but not accurate, because more than one link connects the Herodian period with the Hellenistic age.

When Herod was king of Judea Augustus became the ruler of the Roman world. This was a period of world peace and of great prosperity in which Judea fully shared. Being one of the important terminals in the Indo-Arabian spice trade, the treasury of the kingdom filled to the brim. Like other rulers of local states in Asia Minor and Syria, Herod embarked on ambitious architectural undertakings, which provided labor for all. The crown of Herod's undertakings was no doubt the rebuilding of the Second Temple, the beauty of which was praised by friend and foe.

The prosperity lasted for a few generations only. The Temple was burnt down by the Romans and razed to the ground in subsequent periods, but some if its grandeur has been recovered in the recent excavations in Jerusalem still in progress. For the construction of the walls surrounding the Temple Mount the hardest obtainable stone was employed, of which the high quality architectural designs were made too. Even the inscriptions directing priests to their posts show the delicacy of this work. The inscriptions were generally written in Hebrew, but there were also some in Greek, for the instruction of foreigners.

Opposite the Temple Mount, to the west, was the Upper City, where lived the richer class of Jerusalemites. Although in the middle of the metropolis, the houses were spacious, paved with mosaics, their walls stuccoed and painted. The paintings were made in the fashion of imitation-marble, as was common in the Roman world at that time, and were it not for a rare occurrence of the seven branched menorah found in one of the rooms and a ritual bath in another, it would be difficult to distinguish between this house and the villa of a rich Roman citizen anywhere. These houses were lavishly furnished and equipped with good quality locally made stone basins, bowls and tables.

The prosperity of Jerusalem in the 1st century AD was expressed not only by the high standard of living of its inhabitants, but also in the tombs provided for the dead. Unique in their grandeur are the three rock-cut monuments standing almost intact to this very day in the Valley of Kedron to the southeast of the Temple Mount, the so-called Tomb of the Kings to the north of the city, and scores of other tombs all around it. Due to the costliness of burial space the bones were regularly transferred after some time into beautifully decorated stone ossuaries, thousands of which have been found in and around Jerusalem.

Miniature model of the Second Temple with the city of Jerusalem seen in the background.

An unrolled slip of the *Tefilin*, containing verses from the Pentateuch, found at Qumran, site of the Dead Sea scrolls.

Herod's building activities were by no means limited to Jerusalem alone. The king fortified Judea with a chain of fortresses and fortified palaces on the southern and eastern borders. Most important of these and best preserved were the fortresses of Herodium, which Herod chose as his burial-place, and the palaces at Masada, the beauty of which is beyond imagination. These are only two of a chain of palaces which the king built in the region of Jericho. Herod rebuilt Caesarea Maritima, which lay in ruins, naming the new city after his benefactor Caesar Augustus, embellishing the city with temples, palaces, a theater, a huge harbor, and supplying it with running water brought from afar. Another city which Herod rebuilt was ancient Samaria, which he renamed Sebaste, in honor of the same Roman emperor. On the acropolis of Samaria Herod erected a large temple, dedicated to the cult of the emperor, while at the foot of the mountain he built a new wall and a formidable gate.

THE JEWISH WAR.   The years preceding the destruction of the Temple were a time of religious and social unrest. The completion of the Temple and other public works meant harder times for thousands of people who were previously engaged on their construction. Herod's death in 4 BC only aggrevated the situation, and the internal social, religious and cultural strife worsened. Some Jewish sects, like the Essenes, withdrew into the solitude of the Judean Desert facing the Dead Sea, where they founded the community of Qumran, possibly biblical Ir-melah, where the scribes of the sect copied the books of the Bible and the sages of the sect laid down its rules.

The Qumran community was founded during the time of John Hyrcanus or in the early days of Alexander Jannaeus and lasted until the destruction of the Second Temple. According to the writing of the sect — our main source for its history — it was founded by the Teacher of Righteousness, who revealed his ideas to the small sect by expounding the prophesies of the prophets of former times. Bitter controversy raged between the sect and its adversaries, at the head of whom stood the False Preacher and the Evil Priest. This latter man is described as a mighty ruler who oppressed the Teacher of Righteousness. These events possibly took place in the early Hasmonean period, on the eve of the foundation of the settlement of the Qumran sect. The members of the sect were a group of religious extremists, active at the time of the Second Temple, ardently expecting the End of Days. In order to achieve their aims they chose to live in the desert. The basic principles of the sect were to return to the truth, to refrain from any defiling contact with outsiders, and to live in the desert. They led a fully communal life, the novices obeying their superiors. Qumran seems to have been one of a chain of settlements of adherents of this sect. It is thought that this sect is identical with the Essenes, referred to by Josephus Flavius and by Pliny.

There were also messianic currents, one of which had its beginning in the crucifixion of Jesus by the order of Pontius Pilate, the Roman procurator. The unrest was deepened by the tension between the Jewish and non-Jewish populations of the mixed cities, a tension in which the Romans sided with the non-Jews.

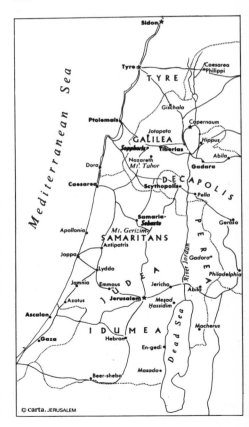

The Holy Land in the time of Jesus.

Thus a series of provocative acts led groups of Jewish extremists to resort to arms in order to fight the Roman Empire. The independent Jewish authorities expressed their autonomy by striking their own silver and bronze coins, replacing the Roman imperial silver, and the local provincial bronze. The Jewish War did not last more than five years. The Romans conquered the Galilee, devastated the country, burnt down Jerusalem and the Temple and rooted out the remnants of the rebels who had found shelter in the fortresses of the desert. Masada, the last Jewish fortress, was conquered by the Romans on May 2, 73 AD.

THE BAR KOHBAH REVOLT.   The second and last Jewish uprising took place in 132 AD. After several generations without Jerusalem, where Hadrian now attempted to found the Roman colony of Aelia Capitolina, and to replace the ruins of the Jewish Temple with a pagan shrine to Jupiter Capitolinus, the Jews, under the leadership of Simon Bar Cosibah (Bar Kohbah, the Son of the Star), conquered Jerusalem, fortified Betthar, Masada and Herodium. Again the Jewish authorities coined in silver and bronze, attempting to reassert Jewish independence. This time the war lasted for little more than three years. The Romans rushed in troops from all over the world, and by 135 AD the last traces of resistance had been crushed by blood and fire.

RECOVERY IN THE LATE ROMAN AND BYZANTINE PERIODS
Both Roman sources and Jewish writings describe the outcome of the Bar Kohbah Revolt as a complete devastation of the country. It seems, however, that these descriptions are highly exaggerated, for the recovery was speedy. It seems

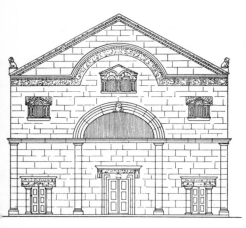

Reconstruction of the synagogue's façade at Capernaum. 3rd century AD.

King David, dressed in Byzantine royal garments, and playing the harp, is depicted on the mosaic floor found in the nave of the ancient synagogue at Gaza, Tell Harube. Above the instrument are the Hebrew letters of "David". 6th century AD.

that the destruction affected mainly the region of Aelia Capitolina, where Jews had been banned anyway after 73 AD. The amount of Jewish remains found at Jerusalem datable to the period following the Bar Kohbah War is minimal, consisting of a single Jewish inscription and a few Jewish lamps. But even they attest to the Jewish determination never to give up Jerusalem and to bewail its ruin. In other parts of the country, by contrast, the Jews thrived, even in mixed cities such as Caesarea, Beth Shean and many others.

THE CONSTRUCTION OF SYNAGOGUES.   By the 3rd century AD the wounds had healed completely. During this period the Jews were already established in the region of Judea south of Bethlehem. The Galilee was entirely Jewish, and so was the Golan adjacent to the Sea of Galilee to the east and the Valley of Jezreel to the south. There were also large Jewish communities in the mixed cities along the Mediterranean coast. In the Valley of Jezreel there flourished the Jewish town of Beth Shearim, where there was a large synagogue, a basilica for the learning of the Law, and an enormous Jewish necropolis to which were brought for burial not only Jews from the Holy Land, but also from the Diaspora. The inscriptions found at Beth Shearim tell of Jews who were brought from as far south as Himyar in Arabia and Palmyra and Phoenicia to the northeast and northwest. The carvings on the walls and the scores of decorated sarcophagi serve as evidence of the quick recovery of the Jewish community in the Holy Land.

From the 3rd century onward scores of Jewish synagogues were built all over the country, in the Galilee, the Valley of Jezreel, the south, the coastal plain and even in the Golan to the northeast and at Gerasa in Provincia Arabia.

CHRISTIANITY IN THE HOLY LAND

During the first two centuries of the new faith Jews comprised a great part of the young Christian community. However, after the bloody crushing of the Bar Kohbah Revolt the schism between Judaism and Christianity became final, and from that time on Christianity strengthened its ranks mainly through converts from the larger pagan towns and through soldiers of the Roman army stationed on the borders of the province. This change is well manifested in the shift from the Aramaic language, spoken by both Jews and early Christians, to the Greek, the language of the non-Jewish population. From the middle of the 4th century AD the schism is also reflected in the distribution of synagogues and churches. While the Galilee, the upper Jordan Valley, the Golan and the southern part of the mountains of Hebron remained basically Jewish, the regions of Aelia Capitolina, the shores of the Sea of Galilee and the coastal plain were mainly Christian.

The Christians must have possessed prayer houses during the first three centuries of their existence, but these are not easily recognized. Such a house was probably the one recently discovered at Capernaum, identified as the house of St Peter. However, the earliest Christian basilicas were not built until after the recognition of Christianity as the state religion. After 324 AD Constantine the Great and his mother Helena made it their policy to celebrate the victory of Christianity by constructing magnificent churches. The earliest were built in Jerusalem, embracing in one large building both the tomb of Jesus and Golgotha, while the Church of the Ascension was constructed on the Mount of Olives. The Church of the Nativity was built at Bethlehem on the site of the Grotto of the Nativity, and a smaller building was erected at Mambre near Hebron, replacing a pagan temple of the time of Hadrian, on the site where by tradition Abraham sat under the oak. During the same century, or perhaps at the beginning of the next, there were churches built along the shores of the Sea of Galilee, commemorating the miracles of Jesus at *Heptapegon* (the Church of the Loaves and Fishes) and at Gergesa (at the site of the driving out of the devils; of *Matth. 8:28–32*, etc), on the opposite, eastern shore. The number of churches built in the subsequent centuries of which ruins have been discovered is already over 200.

Apart from churches, a large number of monasteries were also built. At the beginning, in the 4th century AD, these were mostly located in the desolate regions of the Judean desert, the Negev and the Sinai.

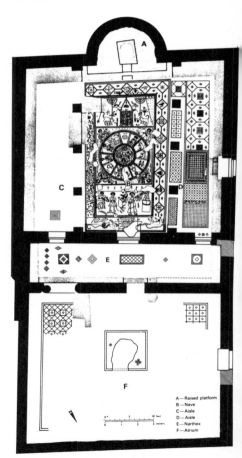

Plan of the hall and elaborate mosaic floors of Beth Alpha synagogue. 6th century AD.

A — Raised platform
B — Nave
C — Aisle
D — Aisle
E — Narthex
F — Atrium

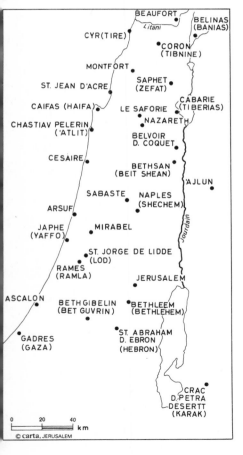

The Crusader Kingdom in the Holy Land. 1099–1291.

BEAUFORT
CYR(TIRE)
BELINAS (BANIAS)
Litani
CORON (TIBNINE)
MONTFORT
SAPHET (ZEFAT)
ST. JEAN D'ACRE
CABARIE (TIBERIAS)
CAIFAS (HAIFA)
LE SAFORIE
NAZARETH
CHASTIAV PELERIN ('ATLIT)
BELVOIR D. COQUET
CESAIRE
BETHSAN (BEIT SHEAN)
'AJLUN
SABASTE
NAPLES (SHECHEM)
ARSUF
JAPHE (YAFFO)
MIRABEL
Jourdain
ST. JORGE DE LIDDE (LOD)
RAMES (RAMLA)
JERUSALEM
ASCALON
BETHGIBELIN (BET GUVRIN)
BETHLEEM (BETHLEHEM)
ST. ABRAHAM D. EBRON (HEBRON)
GADRES (GAZA)
CRAC D. PETRA DESERTT (KARAK)

0   20   40
km
© carta, JERUSALEM

THE ARAB CONQUEST

The Jewish, Christian and Samaritan communities among whom the country was divided, and who all three shared the large mixed cities, lived peacefully throughout the Byzantine period (the Samaritans did revolt several times during this period, but did not suffer severely). This harmony was now to come to an end, and all three communities suffered a change in fortunes. Between the years 636–640 the whole of the Holy Land was conquered by the Moslems. While in the Byzantine period all creeds had been equal before the law, the Moslems made a distinction between 'believers' (themselves) and the 'infidels', this designation applying mainly to the Christians, who were now forced to pay the humiliating 'Dog Tax'. This change upset the stability of the Holy Land. Synagogues were still built and repaired during the first centuries of Moslem rule, but the construction of Christian churches and monasteries ceased completely. The heavy taxation on the 'infidels' caused a speedy depopulation of the country. The desert of the Negev was abandoned first. Then the Sharon plain and the Valley of Jezreel turned into large swamps.

Jerusalem fell to the Moslems in 637 AD; it was the intention of the conquerors to make the Holy City into a shrine rivaling those of Mecca and Medina. In order to achieve this Caliph Abdul Malik (687–691 AD) constructed the Dome of the Rock on the supposed site of the Temple. In its construction were employed materials taken from the Christian churches, and most probably Byzantine artists who mastered the art of mosaics. This is obvious both from the architectural order employed and, mainly, from an analysis of the mosaic art. However, contrary to contemporary Byzantine art, there are no human figures or animals represented in these early Moslem mosaics of the Dome of the Rock and the contemporary el Aqsa mosque, which was erected nearby on the Temple Mount.

THE CRUSADER PERIOD

On July 15th, 1099 Jerusalem was captured by the Crusaders and one year later Baldwin was crowned king of the Latin Kingdom of Jerusalem. The Crusader movement drew forces from a great part of western and central Europe. At different times there came knights from England, France and Germany, while from Pisa and Genoa in Italy came the navies, which played an important role in keeping the lines of communication between Europe and the East open. In order to establish their hold on the Holy Land the Crusaders embarked on an ambitious plan of construction all over the country. Fortresses were built at strategic points, and churches which had been destroyed by the Moslems, or had fallen into disuse, were now rebuilt, and new ones were built also. These churches took the form of small independent fortresses. As the manifest goal of the Crusaders was the recovery of the Holy Sepulchre, this holiest Christian shrine in the Holy Land was attended to as well. Although on a much smaller scale than the original Constantine church, the building was consolidated and a new portal built.

Crusader architecture in the Holy Land was forceful and sturdy, as is attested by the Church of St Ann in Jerusalem, one of the best preserved in the Holy Land; the fortress of Belvoir; of Caesarea; Jeziret Farun at the northern part of the Gulf of Elath; and the spacious hall in St Jean d'Acre. In contrast to the excellent construction of military and civic buildings, Crusader architectural decoration in the Holy Land is rather poor.

Head of Crusader knight sculpted in stone, from the fortress of Montfort.

In order to maintain their hold on the Holy Land during the 250 years of their eastern adventure, the Crusaders were forced to send no less than eight crusades. Despite the great efforts of Louis IX, king of France, the leader of the last two crusades, the Kingdom of Jerusalem collapsed and in 1260 the founder of the Mameluk dynasty, Baibars, began a systematic destruction of the Crusader fortresses. The last Crusader fortress in the Holy Land, Acre, was evacuated in 1291 AD.

We have summarily reviewed above the highlights of pre- and biblical archaeology in the Holy Land, from earliest times to the end of the Crusader period. Shortly after that period the Holy Land became a remote, desolate and unimportant province of the large Turkish Empire. The most prosperous parts of the country, the Valley of Jezreel, the Jordan Valley and the coastal region extending from Acre in the north to as far as Jaffa in the south, turned into malaria infested swamps; the woods which once covered the mountainous parts of the country were all felled; the roads filled with robbers, and the desert, which hitherto was arrested by human effort at the southern extremity of the country, now encroached on most of it. The remnant of the original population clung to the Holy Cities, keeping the glowing ashes alive, until the revival of the 19th century.

AVRAHAM NEGEV

CHRONOLOGICAL TABLE

25000–10000 B.C.

PALAEOLITHIC (OLD STONE AGE)   Prehistory. Cave-man culture. Hunting and fishing.

10000–7500

MESOLITHIC (MIDDLE STONE AGE)   Prehistory. The Natufian culture. Beginning of agriculture. Domestication of dogs. Dry climate in the Holy Land. First artistic expression. Jericho, the first fortified city.

7500–4000

NEOLITHIC (NEW STONE AGE)   Prehistory. Yarmukian culture. Production of pottery. Earliest villages. Hoe cultivation. Domestication of sheep, cattle, goats and pigs. Fertility cults. Climate in the Holy Land stabilizes, and from this period on, remains unchanged.

4000–3150

CHALCOLITHIC   Prehistory. Ghassulian culture. Discovery of copper. Round square houses, and subterranean dwellings in agricultural settlements.

3150–2200

EARLY BRONZE AGE   Canaanite Period. Beth-Yerah culture. Flourishing urban culture. Development and diffusion of writing. Increase in population. Urban settlement mainly in plains (Gezer) and the Jordan Valley (Beth-Yerah). Law codification in Mesopotamia. Epic, dramatic and religious literature in Mesopotamia and Egypt. International trade routes crossing Canaan, bringing about Egyptian and Mesopotamian influences.

2200–1550

MIDDLE BRONZE AGE   Small city-states of Western Semites. The Age of the Patriarchs. Hyksos invasion of Canaan and Egypt. Metal arms and tools. Horse and war-chariot introduced into Canaan and Egypt by Hyksos. Beginning of alphabetical script in Sinai and Canaan. Amorites, Hittites and other Semitic nomads, penetrate Canaan.

1550–1200

LATE BRONZE AGE   Canaanite fortified city-states. Canaan under Egyptian rule. The Exodus; beginning of the Israelite invasion of Canaan. Birth of the Hebrew nation. Moses and Joshua.

1200–1000

IRON AGE   Israelite Period. Israelite conquest of Canaan. The Philistines ("Sea Peoples") invade Canaan and establish their cities along the coast. The Israelites struggle with the Phillistines. The period of the Judges. Diffusion of alphabetical writing.

1000–900

THE KINGDOM OF ISRAEL   David conquers Jerusalem (c. 1000). Solomon builds the First Temple and city walls in Jerusalem (c. 960). Organization of Israelite states. Economic prosperity: mining, foreign trade, construction. Political and geographical expansion of Israel. The kingdom divides into Judah and Israel (928).

900–586

THE FALL OF ISRAEL AND JUDAH   Phoenician and Aramean influences. Intensive development of Israelite and Judean culture. The great prophets in Samaria and Jerusalem. The Assyrians conquer Samaria. Exile of Israel (722). Nebuchadnezzar of Babylon destroys Jerusalem. Jews exiled to Babylon (586).

586–332

PERSIAN PERIOD   The return from Babilonian captivity begins in the reign of Cyrus (537). Construction of the Second temple begins. Judah becomes a Persian province — Yehud. Rule of the High Priests and the "Great Assembly" at Jerusalem.

332–152

HELLENISTIC PERIOD   Alexander the Great of Macedon conquers the Persian Empire, but leaves Jerusalem untouched. Hellenization in Judah. Foundation of Hellenistic cities. The *Septuagint* — the first translation of the Bible into Greek. Religious persecution of the Jews by Antiochus Epiphanes, who sacks Jerusalem and plunders the Temple. The Maccabees reconquer the city and rededicate the Temple (164).

152–37

HASMONEAN PERIOD   Hasmonean Dynasty (141–63). Independent Jewish state (up to 63). Jerusalem under Roman control (63). Herod the Great appointed king of the Jews by the Romans (40). Reconstruction of the Temple (20). Strong influence of Roman culture. Material prosperity and spiritual turmoil.

37 BC–70 AD

ROMAN (HERODIAN) PERIOD   Pontius Pilate procurator of Judea. Jesus Christ. The Jews revolt against Roman oppression. The Great Revolt culminates in the fall of Jerusalem and the destruction of the Second Temple by Titus (70).

70–324

ROMAN PERIOD   Fall of Masada (73). The Jews led by Bar Kokhba drive out the Romans and again make Jerusalem the Jewish capital (132). The Emperor Hadrian destroys Jerusalem and builds a new walled city — Aelia Capitolina, with a temple dedicated to Jupiter (135). Judea is named Palestina by Hadrian (135). Jewish villages flourish in the Galilee. The Mishnaic and Talmudic era. New spiritual center at Yavne and in the Galilee.

324–640

BYZANTINE PERIOD   Constantine conquers Jerusalem, thereby inaugurating the first Christian rule over the city (326). Persian invasion (614). Moslem invasion (630). End of Byzantine rule.

640–1099

EARLY ARAB PERIOD   Erection of the Dome of the Rock (691).

1099–1291

THE CRUSADER PERIOD   Establishment of the Latin kingdom and Crusader Jerusalem (1099).

The Southern and the Western walls of the Temple Mount in Herodian times. A reconstruction. To the left (west) is depicted a stairway leading up to the gate of the Royal Stoa. To the right (south) are seen the Huldah gates.

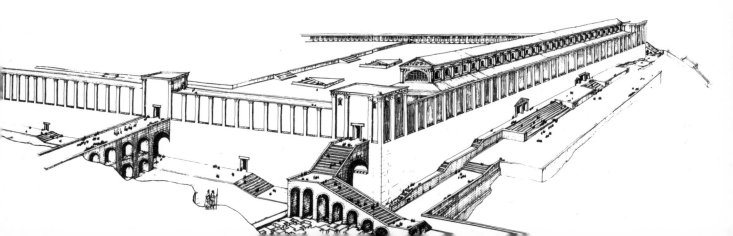

In the caves of ancient man, on the slopes of Mount Carmel overlooking the Mediterranean Sea, are preserved relics of prehistoric civilizations over 150,000 years old. Originally, these caves housed groups of hunters and food-gatherers resembling Stone Age Man, but about 12,000 years ago they gave place to the first tillers of the soil, belonging to the early *Natufian* culture. When the Natufian culture began to spread over the country, man began to leave the caves in search of more suitable habitation.

The prehistoric men living in these caves, left rich relics behind — the earliest tools made by man, including stone bowls, scythe-blades made of flint, and fishing spears and hooks made out of bone. Also the very earliest beginning of man's architecture can be seen in the floors and ancient walls. To the astonishment of archaeologists, excavations have uncovered in this area the first example of man as an artist: tools with carved handles, necklaces of shell, ornaments made from bone, and also a man's head sculpted in chalkstone. The botanical and zoological remains which have survived show man's first discovery of agriculture.

There have been various expeditions digging in these caves since 1929. One of the caves — *the Tannur* or *Tabun* — the Cave of the Oven — pictured here — became famous for the skeleton it contained, known as 'the woman of Tabun'. These diggings provided a detailed picture of man's remarkable advance in his material, religious and artistic culture, as well as of the variegated animal world, and of the harsh climatic conditions prevalent in the area in ancient times.

Traces of the cultures of prehistoric man, dating from over 500,000 years ago, were discovered in Tel Ubeidiya, situated 23 km south of the Sea of Galilee, on the bank of the River Jordan 205 m below sea-level (L). Hundreds of artifacts were found, and remains of more than one hundred animals, many of which have already vanished from the face of the earth. The excavations in Tel Ubeidiya are still in progress.

The Natufian culture marked a truly revolutionary era, offering the first evidence of man's spiritual concerns, such as the importance which man attached to burial. This contracted skeleton, with a string of beads around the head, was discovered in the Cave of the Valley, on Mount Carmel.

Cultural processes which began in the Natufian culture are seen in a more advanced form in the Pre-Pottery Neolithic period at Jericho. This may be seen in the burial of sculpted skulls below the floors of houses, which attests to the presence of an ancestor cult (R).

2|3|4

It is possibly due to the severe
conditions of life during most
of the Prehistoric period that
we find so few works of art.
The life of the food-gatherer
and hunter left too little time
for leisure. This seems
gradually to have changed
during the comparatively short
period of the Natufian culture.
Too little is known of the
purpose of art in these early
periods. It is possible that
what we consider to be artistic
expressions had more of a
magical, protective value, as is
the case with this bone
necklace found in the Cave of
the Valley on Mount Carmel.

|5

The Lady from Horevat Minha. This site, situated some 15 km south of the Sea of Galilee, has been occupied since the Pre-Pottery Neolithic period. Remains of the earlier phases of occupation are scant, but in the latest phase of the Pre-Pottery period there was already one large round building on the site, of 20 m diameter. In the Pottery-Neolithic phase the inhabitants lived in small huts, in fact pits of eliptic shape, 3.5 m long. The settlers of Horevat Minha were farmers, depending for survival on the elements, on the fertility of the land, and on their domesticated animals. It is for this reason that the fertility cult was of such great importance. This female figurine, one of several, exaggerates the size of the reproductive organs. Similar, but much more numerous, were the finds of fertility figurines in the large contemporary village of Shaar Hagolan.

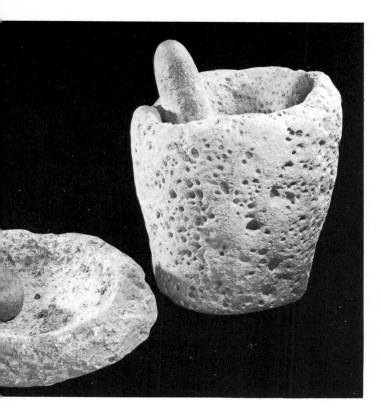

Jericho, presumably the first city in history as well as the first city conquered by the Israelites, has always been a most attractive target for the various invaders who wished to take advantage of its location as a crucial stronghold. It controlled one of the few roads leading from east to west, crossing the River Jordan, at the north of the Dead Sea, and was also an oasis in the midst of the barren desert. In order to defend the city against potential invaders, a huge wall was erected to surround the city. The diameter of the tower, seen here, which was built into the wall, reaches 8.5 m and its height rises to 7.75 m. In its center is located a staircase leading from the city to the roof of the tower. This tower is an impressive monument and a considerable architectural achievement. During the Pre-Pottery Neolithic period, Jericho was a densely populated town, extending over an area of 10 acres. The construction of wall and towers indicates a highly developed and well-organized society, and a prosperous urban life, quite outstanding for as early a period as the 8th century BC.

The production of food was responsible, to a great extent, for the rise of urbanization and for the expansion of rural settlements throughout the fertile and well-watered parts of the Holy Land. In order to produce food, a larger variety of tools was needed than those which the food-gatherer and hunter possessed. Hoes were needed for working the land, and they were made of stone attached to a stick (R). For reaping the harvest flint knives and sickles were used (Bottom), and the grain finally crushed in stone pestles (L).

Some of the most important discoveries in the Holy Land have been made in the deserts surrounding the country. In ancient times they were a safe refuge, whereas in modern times both their climatic properties and their distance from the settled country, have helped to preserve organic materials from decay, and metal objects from theft. This was how the unimaginably rich Cave of the Treasure was preserved for posterity. The cave is situated on a precipitous rock, one thousand feet high and access is very difficult. The most important part of the treasure consisted of 429 copper objects, for many of which science has had to invent names. This was also the case for the rod, decorated by gazelles' heads, possibly used in some unknown ritual (Chalcolithic Period).

The Early Bronze Age, which lasted one thousand years, saw great prosperity in the Holy Land. Scores of cities and hundreds of villages were settled in the fertile plains of the country. Prosperity also meant better and more varied types of pottery. At Beth Yeraḥ, one of the largest and most important sites from the Early Bronze age, situated at the southwest corner of the Sea of Galilee, a new type of pottery was identified. This type was produced in the second phase of this long period, and includes large bowls, well burnished, red on the inside and black on the outside. Sometimes these bowls are decorated by incisions.

11

Man of the Chalcolithic period must have felt like a bird spreading its wings for the first time. The acquisition of copper, easy to shape into any desired form, enabled him to produce tools for almost any need. Better tools meant better living, and also more leisure.

This is the only explanation for the sudden appearance of such variety in artistic expression. Ivory carving was only one of the new artistic processes. Figurines in ivory were made of men, women, human heads, animals and birds. Realism was achieved by implanting hair in holes made in the head, face, and other parts of the body. Eyes were frequently inlaid. These figurines originate in Beersheba.

12 | 13 | 14

The spiritual wealth of people in the Chalcolithic period is even more noticeable in the cults connected with death. Great importance was attached to after-life, and for this reason care was taken to ensure that the bones should be collected properly, in order to be preserved for eternity. The practice of bone-collection probably originated at a time when the society which practised it was at the stage of settling down. Part of the community was still wandering with flocks, while others attended to the fields. Should a shepherd die far away from home, his bones would be collected after some time and placed at the tribal cemetery in a clay container in the shape of a house, thus giving us some indication of the style of dwellings at that time. The largest cemetery of this period in the Holy Land was discovered in a cave at Azor, in the vicinity of Jaffa. The containers, called ossuaries, were also made in shapes other than houses, such as jars.

The larger cities of the Holy Land during the Early Bronze Age were located in the fertile valley. This was also the case of Megiddo, first settled in the Chalcolithic period on the border of the Valley of Jezreel. At an early stage of the Early Bronze Age, a shrine was built there (L). It was round, and built out of small field stones, a practice which was still known in biblical times: "If you make an altar for me, you must not build it of hewn stone." (*Ex. 20:25*). It is 8 m in diameter, 1.40 m high, and approached by steps to the east. At this site temples were later built throughout the Canaanite period.

Tel Beth Shean dominates two very fertile valleys, the Valley of Jezreel on the west, and the Jordan Valley on the east. Like Megiddo, it was first settled in the Chalcolithic period. During the Bronze Age it was an important Canaanite city and an Egyptian stronghold for the north of the country. Numerous temples have been discovered on this mound, mainly from the Late Bronze Age, to which period also belong numerous written records in Egyptian Hieroglyphic script. Beth Shean, the Arabic name of which was Tell el Husn — the Mound of Strength — was one of the last cities conquered by the Israelites.

Gezer was one of the most important Canaanite strongholds in the coastal plain, one of the six most important cities in the Land of Canaan, and later of the the royal cities of King Solomon. By the later phases of the Middle Bronze Age it was already an important cultic center. This row of upright pillars, standing in the middle of the mound (L), is most probably the *Massebot* of the Bible, the high-place, which formed an essential part of the Canaanite cult.

The Holy Land prospered greatly during the Middle Bronze II period, when the whole of the ancient Near East was ruled by the Hyksos. This prosperity is reflected in the richness of contemporary tombs. The dead person would be placed on a wooden couch, well supplied with food, drink, and jewellery. Warriors would be provided with weapons, and women with cosmetic implements. The drinking-cup in the form of a man's head was found in a tomb from that period at Jericho.

18 | 19 | 20

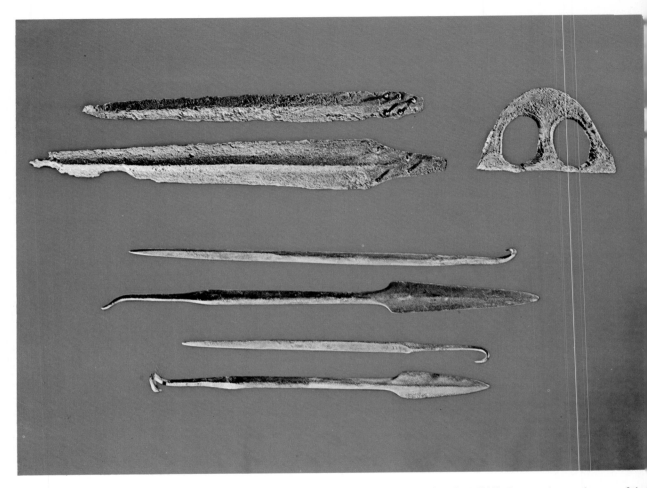

New weapons, indicating a marked advance in the art of war, were introduced during the Middle Bronze Age — the age of the biblical Patriarchs. These weapons gave rise to new tactics particularly in the system of fortification. The horse-drawn war-chariot and the battering-ram, were introduced during this period. The introduction of these new elements permitted the development of better arms both for attack and defense, in the open field, and in face-to-face engagements in built-up areas. In this way the spears and lances were made longer, and with flat flanges, to achieve better piercing and cutting-power. The hinged ends secured a better holding in the wooden shaft. The "eye" axe, of a type found at Megiddo, was made to cut through the bronze helmets protecting the heads of warriors.

The mold for casting images of Ashera, the goddess of the sea, found in a large Middle Bronze road-shrine at Nahariya is unique. It was made of stone, 22 cm long and 7 cm wide, and depicts a naked woman wearing a conical, horned head-dress. The shrine itself consisted of a 11×6 m building (replacing an older, smaller one) and a circular high-place, 6 m in diameter. Hundreds of pottery vessels were found there (Overleaf) and also a large quantity of silver and bronze jewellery, offerings made to the gods. Some of these objects were cast at a workshop in the temple precinct.

Only a small fraction of the types found in the Canaanite temple at Nahariya is represented in the pottery here. The temple in which these finds were made was used over a comparatively short period of time, and once it was abandoned at the end of the Middle Bronze Age, the site was never occupied again. It is for this reason mainly that the finds, including fragile pottery, were so well-preserved. There are numerous vessels in which food and drink were served to the goddess, as well as small vessels and figurines which were also offered as presents to the goddess. It is possible that in the miniature seven cups, seven different odiferous substances were placed (L).

This mask (R) was found in a Late Bronze Age temple in the lower city of Hazor. In this part of the mound there was an extremely large stone altar, around which were scattered various cult objects, belonging to a temple which was probably destroyed by the Israelites. Among these finds was a bronze standard decorated with snakes, an animal frequently portrayed in cult vessels of the ancient world. This mask, and probably also the standard, were used in a solemn procession, the mask covering the priest's face.

The Canaanite temple of Hazor. When Hazor was conquered by the Israelites, it was described as "formerly the head of all these kingdoms" *(Josh. 11:10)*. The city, one of the most important in the ancient Near East, was frequently mentioned in Egyptian records. The lower city had been occupied, since the beginning of the Bronze Age, whereas in the Middle Bronze Age the rulers of Hazor chose the nearby mound as their fortress. Due to their greater antiquity the temples of Canaanite Hazor were all built in the lower city. Because of the large size of this city, temples were constructed at its northern part as well as in the southwestern corner of the site. The steles, presented here (L), belong to this later temple. One of these steles — all are made of basalt — shows a pair of hands raised in adoration to the sun and moon. The seated figure is probably a king or god. The orthostate of the lion, also of basalt, was found in a third, eastern temple, dating back to the end of the Late Bronze Age, on the eve of the Israelite conquest.

The Canaanite Pantheon was extremely large, and much richer than in the biblical description. Apart from the major deities, the creators and masters of the world, there was also a host of local deities and of deities with lesser functions. They were made of every material: gold, silver, bronze, wood and clay. The Canaanite rulers very frequently engaged in war, and a number of deities were responsible for that activity. Reshef, to whom this figurine from Megiddo is ascribed, was one of them. He is seen brandishing a sword, and protecting his head with a square shield.

25 | 26

The Megiddo Gilgamesh epic and the Beth Shean stele are remnants, found in the Holy Land, of neighboring cultures of the Late Bronze Age. Apart from being an age of great prosperity the Late Bronze Age was also one of learning. To be sure the art of writing was not an art mastered by everybody. This knowledge involved many years of study, learning either the Accadian cuneiform script — the international language of that age — or the Egyptian hieroglyphic writing, which was no less complicated. For this reason religious writing was mastered by priests only, whereas diplomatic and commercial communication was in the hands of scribes. This fragment of the epic of Gilgamesh (L), the Babylonian story of the creation, written in Accadian, is a chance find, discovered by a shepherd who was tending his flock in the vicinity of the mound of Megiddo, many years after the cessation of the archaeological excavations there. The Egyptian stele (R) is of King Seti I (late 14th century BC) and is one of several found in the temples of Beth Shean.

At times, one single find can embody a world of details for an archaeologist, and of such type is this crater from Tel Nagila, which is a large mound located in the southern part of the coastal plain, 28 km east of Gaza. Like numerous mounds in the Holy Land, it was inhabited continuously from the Chalcolithic period onwards, in this case until medieval times. It was a place of considerable importance during the Hyksos period. Although the beginning of the Late Bronze Age was a time of decline for Tel Nagila (the ancient name of this place is still unknown), the ceramic finds of this period are comparatively rich. The crater presented here is of a class known by the name Bichrome ware, as the paintings were in two colors, black and red. The surface of the vessels decorated in this technique was divided into metopes in which animals or birds were painted. It is believed that the potters who produced this type of pottery worked at Tell el Ajjul (Beth Eglaim) on the Mediterranean coast, due west of Tel Nagila.

Ornaments of rare beauty, revealing a high degree of artistic craftsmanship were discovered at Tell el Ajjul, on the seashore, south of Gaza. This site has been identified as the major Canaanite port Beth Eglaim, one of the most flourishing cities in the country. This site had not been settled before the beginning of the Middle Bronze Age. When the Hyksos obtained control of the site, they built a city 30 acres large. Among the discoveries on the mound is a palace belonging to the local rulers, and some sections of Middle and Late Bronze Age streets and houses. Of major importance were three separate large cemeteries discovered to the east of the mound, two of which were from various phases in the Middle Bronze Age, and the third from the Late Bronze Age. The finds in tombs of all these periods were extremely rich, more than in almost any other site in the holy Land. This is especially true of the jewellery. The jewellery collected here comes from several tombs, and includes a bronze mirror and necklaces, earrings and pendants, made of gold and of precious stones, mainly carnelian and agate. Their workmanship testifies to a remarkable imaginative creativity whose beauty is retained to the present day.

Ivory was known in the Near East from the Neolithic period, when it was already a much favored material for the production of carved figures. The main source of elephant tusks was the Sudan, although there were some elephants in Syria and Lebanon as well. In ancient times ivory was one of the most precious materials, and along with gold it was hoarded by kings in their treasuries. In royal houses it was used for the decoration of furniture and jewellery boxes. One of the largest royal treasuries was found in a Late Bronze Age occupation level at Megiddo, which contained objects collected during the Middle and Late Bronze Ages. This jewellery box, 13.05×12 cm, is one of the latest in the treasury, dating back to the 12th century BC. It was decorated by pairs of sphinxes, the *cherubim* of the Bible, on either side, and by individual lions. Both elements were in frequent use throughout the ancient Near East.

31

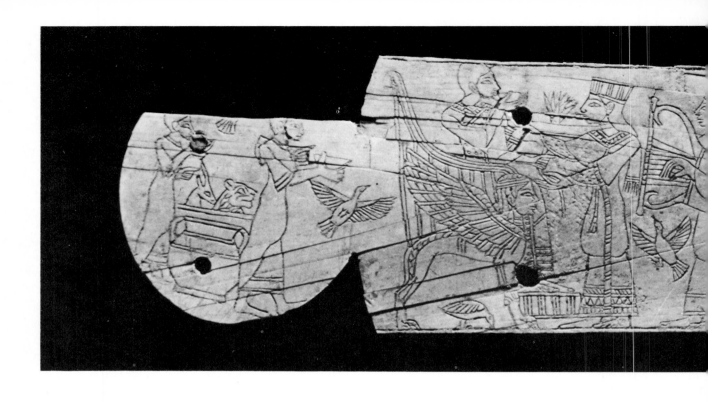

This ivory plaque from Megiddo tells us a two-chapter story. One of the earliest in the Megiddo ivory hoard, this knife-shaped piece is 26 cm long and only 1–1.5 cm thick. In the center of the first story on the left is a king, perhaps the Canaanite king of Megiddo. He is seated on a throne, at both sides of which stand winged sphinxes. The king, bearded, is drinking out of a bowl. In front of the king stands a princess, both the king and the princess wearing embroidered clothing. Behind the princess is a woman playing a nine-stringed lyre, while behind the throne are seen two servants pouring drinks out of a large jar. There is a large platter above the jar with two drinking-vessels shaped in the form of animal heads. Four birds fill in the empty space. On the right there is the scene of a return from a battlefield. This consists of a warrior riding a horse-drawn chariot. There is a boy carrying a sword behind the chariot, two naked, circumcised captives in front of it, and an infantryman armed with a long lance and a round shield. Three plants separate the two chapters of the story.

32

Ashdoda from Ashdod. Ashdod was one of the "five lords of the Philistines" (*Josh. 13:3*). Isolated finds ascribed to the Philistines have been known from many sites since the beginning of our century, but the number of sites at which Philistine occupation levels have been unearthed is still minimal. Ashdod is one of these few sites, and large-scale excavations have been carried out there since 1962. Ashdod was already a town of considerable importance in the Middle Bronze II and Late Bronze Ages. The latest Late Bronze city suffered violent destruction by fire, and on these ashes the earliest Iron Age city was founded by the Philistines. It was a strongly fortified city, as is attested by the large six-bay gate which has been unearthed. No shrine of any kind pertaining to the Philistine city has as yet been discovered, but some of the objects found there must have belonged to some cult. This woman, seated on a throne, perhaps represents a Philistine goddess, whose name is Ashdoda, inspired by figurines of the Mycenean "Great Goddess", the leading goddess of that culture. This is the view of scholars, because the Sea People, of which the Philistines formed part, originated in that part of the Mediterranean.

| 33

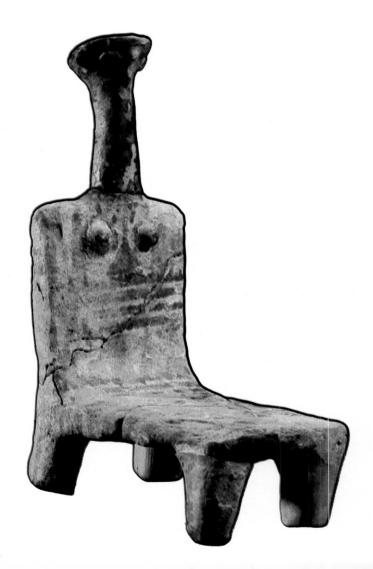

On numerous sites along the Mediterranean coast of the Holy Land, as well as on some sites in the interior of the country, pottery vessels have been found which have been identified as Philistine. They were found in occupation levels dating back to the 12th and 11th centuries BC. Although this Philistine pottery has some affinities with products of the Late Bronze Age, it is certainly an independent group. The vessels more easily recognized as pertaining to the Philistines are large, deep bowls, with horizontal handles (**Foreground** r), the "stirrup-jug" (**Center**) and the "beer-jug" (**Background**), identified as such on account of the strainer with which it was provided, and which is believed to have been used in order to strain the barley. All these vessels resemble Aegean prototypes. Philistine pottery is normally coated by a light-colored slip on which were executed the black and red paintings. Together with geometric patterns, the picture of a swan turning its head or pecking under its wing, was one of the most favored subjects.

34

This anthropoid coffin was discovered some five years ago when illicit diggers at Deir el Balah, some 13 km south of Gaza, found it in a cemetery buried more than 10 m below the sand dunes. The tombs contained unusually large quantities of vessels made of bronze, alabaster, faience, pottery imported from Mycenae, Cyprus and Egypt, gold jewellery and cultic Egyptian figurines. The tombs contained about 50 large anthropoid coffins. These are elongated clay objects, almost man-sized, consisting of a container for the body and a removable cover on which the features of the human face are molded. The hands are always molded on the lower part of the coffin. The finds from this cemetery date back to the later phases of the Late Bronze Age, in the 14th century BC. Years ago similar coffins were discovered in 12th and 11th century cemeteries at Beth Shean in the north, and at Tel Sharuhen in the south of the country. These cemeteries belonged to the Philistines. It thus seems that they acquired this burial practice from the Egyptian nobility, with whom they established contact in the 12th century BC.

Iron Age tools. The separation of iron ore from its oxides is one of the most complicated processes in ancient metallurgy, and for this reason the exploitation of copper and the making of bronze preceded it by thousands of years. Iron in its pure state, of meteoritic origin, was used in Egypt as early as 3,000 BC, but it was not until the 13th century BC that iron ore was purified. This achievement is generally ascribed to the Hittites, whose empire was located in Asia Minor and northern Syria. While on their way to Syria and Egypt the Philistines learned this process from the Hittites. By producing weapons and iron tools, such as those pictured here (R), they were able to overpower their Egyptian adversaries. For several centuries the Philistines rigorously guarded the secret: "No blacksmith was to be found in the whole of Israel, for the Philistines were determined to prevent the Hebrews from making swords and spears. The Israelites had to go down to the Philistines for their ploughshares, mattocks, axes and sickles to be sharpened." (*I Sam. 13:19–20*).

35 | 36

At the beginning of the Iron Age the huge lower city of Hazor was abandoned, possibly after its conquest by Joshua. The new Israelite city (L) was founded on the nearby mound, covering an area of only 30 acres. The earliest Iron Age occupation on the mound dates back to the 12th or 11th century BC. This was nothing more than a small rural settlement. It was king Solomon who made Hazor one of the most important Israelite cities: "This is the record of the forced labor which King Solomon conscripted to build — Hazor, Megiddo, and Gezer." (*I Kings 9:15*). At the foreground of this photograph can be seen the six-bay gate which was constructed by order of King Solomon. Behind the gate is seen the large pillared storehouse dating back to the 9th century BC, when Hazor already formed part of the divided kingdom, belonging to the kingdom of Israel. Further back are seen the citadels built there in the Assyrian, Persian, and Hellenistic periods, when Hazor was the seat of the foreign governors of Galilee. In the middle of the mound can be seen the entrance to the huge water supply system, dating back to the 9th century BC.

Throughout the Israelite period the older Canaanite cults and rituals were by no means extinct. This is well known from the Bible, and the prophets had more than a word to say on the improper behavior of the people in regard to these cults. The attempts made by several kings to abolish the heathen cults met with only partial success. The persistence of these popular cults is well attested by the great number of house-altars, incense-burners, and Astarte figurines such as those seen in this picture.

In deciding on the method of excavation to be used, the archaeologist must make a choice between two contradictory desires — obtaining as full a picture as possible of the site which he is excavating, and learning as much as possible of the history of the site. Because of the large size of most ancient archaeological sites in the Holy Land, the full achievements of both aims is an impossible task. In order to obtain a clear picture, one must excavate a certain stratum, representing a city from a rather limited space in time, or at least excavate part of it. The archaeologist must thus explore a city-date and a section of the city-wall — if indeed the city was fortified. Next, he must examine the ruler's palace, and a temple. Then come at least one or two private dwellings, some workshops, a market, and the water supply system. All of this would be the minimum area of the city required in order to obtain the desired picture. To achieve this would take several seasons of the archaeologist's time. He would then be far from knowing much of the general history of the site. The ideal situation would be to go on "peeling-off" layer after layer until the aim is achieved.

This, however, is impractical. Thus the archaeologist is forced to cut a rather narrow section through the mound — like the one shown here at the Gezer excavation — penetration through all the numerous strata making up the full history of the city, but offering a very blurred picture of the composition of each separate stratum. The skill of the archaeologist lies in his ability to reconcile these two contradictory desires.

| 39

This clay tablet, 7.5×10 cm large, known as the Gezer calendar, is the earliest known document written in ancient Hebrew, dating back to the time of King Solomon. On this tablet were recorded agricultural activities in the order in which they were performed: harvesting, sowing, late sowing, and cutting of flax, harvesting of barley, harvesting and measuring, vintage, and summer fruit.

This incense-burner (L), made of clay, belongs to the Iron Age and was found in "Taanach by the waters of Megiddo." (*Judg. 5:19*). It is built in the form of a tower, decorated by human figures. The incense was burnt in a bowl at the upper part of the burner. Taanach is situated at the northern end of the valley of Jezreel, guarding one of the main passes from the south. It was an important city in the Middle and Late Bronze Ages and frequently mentioned in Egyptian sources as well as in the Bible.

Houses were built in the Holy Land from as early as the Neolithic period. The earliest houses were domed structures, similar in form to the temporary huts of nomadic people. These were made of a stone socle, and mud-brick walls, roofed over by wood. Still within the Neolithic period a house was developed in the form of an oblong hall, fronted by a porch supported by two columns. With minor changes this plan persisted through the Chalcolithic period. A basic change in the planning of the house occurred only in the Middle Bronze Age, at which time more spacious dwellings were built. These consisted of a court-yard around which were grouped rooms, their number depending on the wealth of the household. Better homes had an upper storey, too. This type of house persisted throughout the whole of the Bronze Age, and was also very common in the Iron Age. However, the contribution of the Israelites to house and town-planning was the introduction of the type of house known by the name of Four Space (or room) House, such as the one seen here. It consisted of an oblong court, at the narrow end of which was the entrance to the house. Along three sides of the court there were rooms of the length of the court. The court was partly open to the sky, the roof of the covered part resting on pillars. Sometimes rooms opened onto the court. The roofs were framed, and were made of beams of wood, branches of trees and pounded earth.

Israelite furniture was very simple. Timber was scarce and for this reason cupboards were built into the walls from which stone shelves projected. The table was nothing but a simple mat or skin placed on the floor. On it food and drink were served in a large variety of pottery vessels, made to meet every need.

Beersheba and Arad have both been excavated in recent years. Beersheba had never been a city of importance before the days of the Israelite kingdom, whereas at Arad an Early Bronze Age city was abandoned, and the new Israelite city founded on a higher mound nearby. Both of these sites housed royal fortresses, guarding the southern border of the Judean kingdom, and protecting it from incursions by the Bedouin tribes who inhabited the Negev. This in fact remained the task of both these sites in the Persian, Hellenistic, and Roman periods. Both at Arad and at Beersheba, situated far away from Jerusalem, remains of temples were discovered. The shrine at Arad was a miniature replica of the Temple of Solomon at Jerusalem, whereas at Beersheba (L) a large horned altar was found broken to pieces, and re-used in later construction.

The most important collection of carved ivory in the Holy Land comes from the palace of the Israelite kings at Samaria, to which the prophet Amos referred: "You who loll on beds inlaid with ivory plaques and spread over your couches." The "ivory house" of Ahab is referred to in *I Kings 22:39*. Some of these ivories reflect Egyptian influence and others were inspired by the art of Phoenicia. In the plaque above is seen a lion attacking a bull, a motif much employed in the east until a very late period, while the lower one portrays two sphinxes, a very common feature of Egyptian art. Carving of ivory is one of the earliest arts of mankind, common even in the Natufian culture and in the Chalcolithic and Bronze Age periods. Carved ivory was widely used in Egypt, and in palaces of the Assyrian kings from the 9th and 8th centuries BC.

The Seal of Jehoahaz, Son of the King. The habit of signing documents with a personal seal goes back to early historic times in Mesopotamia and Egypt, from which come thousands of seals in the form of small clay and stone cylinders. Egyptian seals were mostly made in the form of a beatle on the back side, flat on the other. The Israelites borrowed the general form of the seal from the Egyptians, omitting the beatle design. Hebrew seals were mostly made of semi-precious stones, and were inscribed in the ancient Hebrew script, decorated by various animals and birds. An important class of seals is the one belonging to State officials. The seal of Shema, Servant of Jeroboam, found at Megiddo, has been well known for many years (Overleaf), but several others have been discovered since then. Two of these seals deserve special mention: that of Jaazaniahu, Servant of the king, and of Jehoahaz, Son of the king(L), both of which were decorated with almost identical fighting cocks. It is believed that both of these persons belonged to the same distinguished family, from which came State officials, and whose family symbol was the cock.

Stamped jar-handles are found frequently in Judea. These seals were decorated by a double or quadruple winged symbol. Above these appears the world 'lamelek', i.e., 'belonging to the king', and below is one of the four names Hebron, Ziph, Socho and mmsht. These jars were official containers for the payment of taxes in kind. The three names are either of cities in which there were royal potteries, or of cities in which the tax was collected. The fourth title is still somewhat enigmatic, possibly meaning 'of the government'. The seal dates from the 8th and 7th centuries BC.

The seal of Shema the Servant of Jeroboam. The habit of confirming a document with a personal seal goes back to the early history of Mesopotamia, from which come thousands of seals in the form of small clay and stone cylinders, as also from Egypt. The Egyptian seals were mostly made in the form of a beetle on one side, but flat on the other. The Israelites borrowed the general form of the seal from the Egyptians, omitting the beetle design. Hebrew seals are generally made of semi-precious stones. They are inscribed in ancient Hebrew script, and often decorated with pictures of various animals and birds. It is tempting to identify the owner of this seal, found at Megiddo, with an official of Jeroboam.

| 50

Biblical historical literature is austere in its descriptions, and it is only by archaeological finds that a fuller picture of life may be obtained. The score of Hebrew inscriptions inscribed in black ink on potsherds found at Lachish — "The Lachish letters" (L) — is one of the most important literary contributions on the last days of the First Temple period. These letters were written by Hoshayahu, a soldier, subordinate to Yaush, the commander of the garrison at Lachish. This letter, perhaps one of the latest, was written on both sides of the potsherd, the first eight lines of which are shown here: *May Yhwh let my Lord hear even now tidings of good. According to whatever my Lord has sent (=written) thus has thy slave done. I have written on the page according to whatever my Lord has sent to me. And when my Lord has sent about the sleeping house, there is nobody. And Semakhyahu, him has taken Shemayahu and brought him up to the city, and thy slave, my Lord, shall write thither, (asking), where he is;* (on the reverse side): *because in his turning he had inspected, he would now, that for the signal-stations of Lachis we are watching, according to the signs which my Lord gives, because we do not see (the signals of) Azeqah.* Much of the meaning of these letters is still enigmatic.

The Hebrew system of weights (R) as reflected in biblical writings was based on the Babylonian standard of 3,600 shekels to the kikar. In the excavations, and very often on the surface, a large number of stone weights were found, many of which bore an inscription in Hebrew letters. These units were mostly of a half or quarter of a shekel. In *Deut. 25:13* we read: "You shall not have unequal weights in your bag, one heavy, the other light." Archaeological finds indicate that this prescription was not always strictly adhered to.

Tel Dan is one of the most recently excavated sites in the Holy Land, and the excavations are still in progress. Layish, originally Dan, was the northernmost city in the Holy Land. It is situated at the foot of Mount Hermon, in a region rich in springs, rivers, and verdure. Ancient Layish is mentioned in Egyptian and Babylonian sources. The Danites conquered the city and named it after their father. It formed one of the most important centers in the kingdom of Israel, and the temple established there by the Israelite conquerors became one of the most important shrines in the Holy Land, rivaling that of Jerusalem. In the time of Jeroboam (*I Kings 12:29*) the golden calf was set up there. In 732 BC the city was conquered by the Assyrians. In excavations the ramparts of the city in the Early Bronze Age have been unearthed and some remains of the Middle Bronze II period. Most important, however, were the remains of the Israelite city, to which belongs a formidable gate, approached by a paved road, unique in its beauty in the Holy Land (seen in our photograph). This road ultimately reaches an 18.7×18.2 m large platform, built of ashlar, and approached by a monumental flight of steps. It was most probably an open-air sanctuary, perhaps the place at which the golden calf was set up.

| 53

The Siloam tunnel. "[When] (the tunnel) was driven through. And this was the way in which it was cut through: while . . . (were) still . . . axe(s), each man toward his fellow, and while there were still three cubits to be cut through, [there was heard] the voice of a man calling to his fellow, for there was an overlap (or: fissure) in the rock on the right and on the left. And when the tunnel was driven through, the quarrymen hewed (the rock), each man toward his fellow, axe against axe, and the water flowed from the spring toward the reservoir for 1,200 cubits, and the height of the rock above the head(s) of the quarrymen was 100 cubits." This inscription (Above) of the Siloam tunnel (L) was discovered in 1880 at the outlet of Hezekiah's waterways. The Bible recounts this complicated engineering feat in only a few words: "The other events of Hezekiah's reign, his exploits, and how he made the pool and the conduit and brought water into the city, are recorded in the annals of the kings of Judah." (*II Kings 20:20*).

Biblical Mareshah, Marissa of the Hellenistic period, was a Phoenician colony in the region of Idumaea. It was a small townlet, only six acres large, situated in the foothills of the mountains of Hebron, one of the most fertile regions of the Holy Land. Under the leadership of Apolophanes son of Sesmaios, Sydonians settled here some time in the 3rd century BC. This combination of names — the Semitic name of the father and the Greek name of the son — symbolizes the extent to which the new settlers were assimilating. In this way the Phoenician language gave way to Greek, and to decorate his eternal resting-place, he asked that the zoological garden of Alexander the Great in Alexandria should be painted, most probably by an Alexandrian painter. The scene presents a trumpeter walking behind his master, while the master himself is riding a Lebanese horse (so the Greek inscription above informs us). There is a dog running at the feet of the horse. The master has just hunted a leopard. This hunting scene is followed by various animals, birds and fish, some real, others imaginary.

The Hellenistic period is a turning-point in the history of the Holy Land. Although cultural and commercial relations with East and West had already existed in the preceding periods, its conquest by Alexander the Great made the Holy Land part of the Western world. Greek became the most widely spoken and written language, and town-planning, art, and architecture — in fact every aspect of material and cultural life — became deeply influenced by the Greeks. Although the country was producing wine in abundance, large quantities were imported from the Greek islands and from the shores of the Black Sea, mainly from Rhodes, Cos and Chios. This is evinced by the thousands of stamped jar-handles originating from those islands.

A Hoard of Persian Silver. Tell Sharuhen (Tell el-Far'a), where this hoard was found, is situated some 24 km. south of Gaza. It is one of the most important mounds on the southern coastal plain. Sharuhen is mentioned only once in the Bible (*Josh. 19:6*), but figures frequently in Egyptian sources. It was one of the last strongholds of the Hyksos, who for three years resisted the Egyptian siege. To this period belong extensive remains of fortifications and of a large palace. Less well preserved were the remains of the Israelite and Persian cities, both of which, however, were richly represented in the finds of the local cemeteries. Among the finds in the tombs of the Persian period there were remains of furniture in wood and metal, weapons, and much metalware. Among the last mentioned there were silver bowls decorated with pointed leaves, flasks, spoons and a laddel, of types well known elsewhere in the Persian empire.

The return of the Jews to the Holy Land from Babylonian captivity was a very slow process. It began in 538 BC and during the years 519–515 BC there began the construction of the Second Temple, although it was soon interrupted. The 5th and 4th centuries BC saw the growth of the quasi-autonomous state of Judah. During the late 6th and 5th centuries BC Judah was incorporated into the monetary system of the Persian empire, but no local mints were founded before the 4th century BC. On coins struck at Judah the legend appears in ancient Hebrew script, the name Yehud, the name of the satrapy, and of Yehizkiya, its governor. These coins, all of silver, have a bird, generally an owl, on the reverse side, and thus resemble Athenian coinage. The obverse of these coins is either blank, or shows the head of a male, and on one occasion a god seated on a winged chair. Coins of this type are few in number.

There were two periods in the history of the Holy Land when secondary burial was practised. The first was in the Chalcolithic period, which has already been referred to, and the second during the 1st century BC–AD. The reason why this custom was resorted to in the early period is not at all clear, nor is it known why it was performed in the later period either. A regular family tomb consisted of an antechamber and of three small rooms, in each of which there were three loculi, nine in all. At the end of two generations there would be no space available for additional burials. This probably gave rise to the custom of collecting the bones of one, and often two persons into a stone ossuary, which was then deposited in a special chamber, or in any other place within the cave. In decoration the ossuaries ranged from plain boxes to richly decorated ones. Here too the most common motifs were rosettes and flowers, although architectural decoration was often employed as well. In numerous cases, the name of the man whose bones were deposited in the box was written on the sides, as was the case in an important and exciting recent find, an ossuary which contained the bones of *Simon, the builder of the Temple.*

60

Purification by immersion in water is an ancient idea, alluded to frequently in the Bible, usually by the simple term 'washing'. In biblical times it was ordained that priests officiating in the Temple, people who had recovered from certain skin and venereal diseases, men and women who had had sexual intercourse, women after their menstrual period, and men who had consumed unclean food should undergo ablution. This kind of purification, especially before participating in certain religious rituals, was common to all peoples of the ancient Near East. In lieu of medicine, purification by water was the most important prophylactic measure in the ancient world. Originally, natural sources of water were used. However, from the time of the Second Temple, special tanks were constructed for purification, named *miqveh,* or ritual bath, like the ones discovered in Jerusalem, Masada, and other Jewish towns.

זה הקבר והנפש שלאלעזר חניה יועזר יהודה שמעון יוחנן
בני יוסף בן עובד יוסף ואלעזר בני חניה
כהנם מבני חזיר

There is scarcely anything comparable to the Necropolis of Jerusalem for revealing the grandeur of the city during the last century that the Second Temple stood. The four monuments represented here, together with the tombs of the kings, situated in the northern part of the city, along the Kedron valley, form the crown of the funerary art in Jerusalem. These four monuments represent two main periods in the history of local art. On the right is the monument of the priestly family of Hezir, identified by a Hebrew inscription on the facade (Above). The entrance to the tomb consists of a porch of two purely Doric columns, dated by its style to the 2nd century BC. Next to it is the monolithic monument known by the name of the Tomb of Zachariah. It is in fact a solid structure with no burial space in it. It consists of a cube decorated by engaged Ionic columns, surmounted by an Egyptian-style pyramid. This solid structure must have been the memorial of a nearby tomb. The third monument is Absalom's Tomb, as it is called. Its lower part is hewn out of the rock, while the drum and the round tholos above it are made of closely fitted ashlars. The lower cube, again, is Ionic, and above it is a Doric frieze. The last two monuments are a local interpretation of late Hellenistic or early Roman art, in a combination which may be termed "Jewish". The last monument is the tomb of Jehoshaphat. Its decoration consists of a floral gable and a floral door frame. This last type of decoration was especially favored by the Jews of Jerusalem at the end of the Second Temple Period.

62

Herod began the construction of the Temple in about 22 BC. We are told by the ancient authorities that in order to lull the suspicions of the Jewish people, the king prepared beforehand all the materials necessary for its construction. The actual work lasted for 46 years. The construction was executed by 10,000 laborers, of whom one thousand were priests. Of these there were five hundred stone-cutters and an equal number of carpenters. The original size of the Temple Mount was doubled by the construction of enormous retaining walls, most of which have been preserved intact. Two large bridges connected the Temple with the Upper City which lay to the west of it. These are known today as 'Robinson's Bridge' and 'Wilson's Arch'. Two of the ancient gates have been preserved on the southern wall. Of the buildings on the Mount nothing has remained, but we are told that in front of the Temple there was the inner court, the Court of Israel, in which there was the 32-cubit-square altar for burnt offerings, the tables, and the other implements used in the preparation of sacrifices. To the west was the enormous Court of Women around which were chambers and store-houses of spices, salt, etc. The Temple itself had a porch before it leading into the hall. In the hall there were the golden tables of shewbread, a small golden altar for the burning of incense, and the golden seven-branched menorah.

Unique is the appearance of the seven-branched menorah or candelabrum, possibly placed on the coins in order to exhort the people to join forces against the enemies from within and from without. Until the 3rd century AD the menorah hardly occurs on Jewish monuments, the only known exceptions being primitive drawings of menoroth on the walls of a tomb from the time of Alexander Jannaeus in Jerusalem (Jason's Tomb), and the very recent discovery of a menorah on the wall of a private dwelling in Jerusalem (R), dating to the last years of the Second Temple Period.

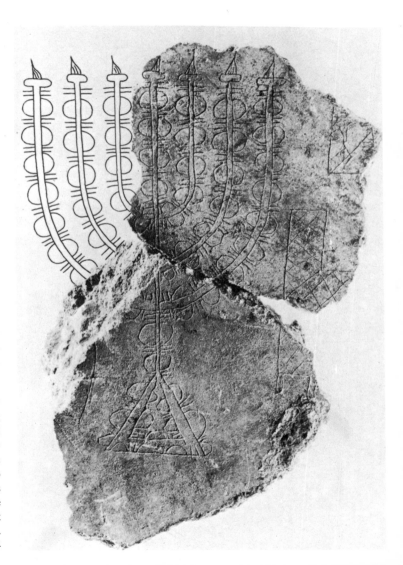

This fragment of a capital was found recently in excavations in the Jewish quarter of Jerusalem. In this part of the Old City there flourished during the times of the Second Temple the Upper City of Jerusalem, in which lived the richer citizens. This capital was made of the excellent local hard limestone, no doubt by local artists. The capital is of the Ionic order and bears evidence of the influence of western culture on local art in the late Hellenistic and early Roman periods. The building from which this beautiful capital came has not yet been discovered.

Jewish art of the Second Temple Period was known mainly from funerary monuments, until recently. From them one may see how deeply influenced the Jews were by Hellenistic and early Roman art. However, the recent Israeli excavations in Jerusalem have slowly brought to light other aspects of Jewish art. Religious inhibitions prevented the Jews from carving images of human beings, animals, and birds, so that their official art, at least, was limited to geometric forms and floral designs, the combined effect of which was very pleasing to the eye

(R).

The growth of international trade, mainly with South Arabia, India, and the Far East, in which Judea took an active part, brought much wealth to the country. It also improved transportation by sea and land, and in this way every novelty created in Rome found its way to the doorstep of every household. If marble was still too dear, furniture was constructed from the excellent, hard Jerusalem limestone, of which even containers and tables were made. In this way the old biblical table in the form of a piece of skin (the Hebrew word for table — *shulhan* — originates from the word 'skin') was replaced by more modern tables of this kind.

The refinement in the conditions of life may also be noted in the pottery of the Herodian period. It was produced in a great variety of types. There were special wares made for the oven and the kitchen, for the table, for cosmetics, for illumination, and for religious purposes. Imports abound, and even the pottery produced locally echoes that of Rome and other provinces. Few types were, however, specifically Jewish, as was the Herodian lamp (Bottom l), of a simple, graceful form, replacing in the Jewish household Roman lamps which were often decorated by offensive scenes.

67 | 68

Until quite recently mosaic art in the Holy Land was known mostly from buildings of the 3rd, 4th and later centuries AD only. However, in the past decade or so, with the commencement of archaeological excavations of sites of the Herodian period, earlier mosaics came to light. First were the mosaics discovered at Herod's palace at Masada, and later came the discoveries in the Jewish Quarter of Jerusalem, where once was the Upper City. Mosaics covered some of the living rooms, bathrooms and corridors leading to water installations.

Contrary to what was customary in the pagan world, where mythology and everyday life were much favored motifs, Jewish mosaic art was completely in keeping with other fields of art employing geometric, floral and formal motifs only, such as the guilloche, crowsteps and the running wave, exemplified in the decoration of the mosaic panel from the Mansion. The compass drawn rosette and the palm leaf also occur frequently in this art. These mosaic floors were made in very small cubes of stone, in black, white and red only; other colors were rarely employed.

The number of private houses from the Roman period excavated in the Holy Land is rather small, and until very recently none was known from Jerusalem. During the past decades, however, several houses have been unearthed in the Upper City of Jerusalem, situated to the west of the Temple Mount, from which one could once admire the glory of the Temple. Outstanding among these houses are two dwellings, one named the "mansion" (R), covering an area of some 600 square meters, and the other known as the "burnt house". The plan of these houses is one common in the Holy Land from early times: a court around which are grouped the rooms of the house. Both of these houses were destroyed by the conflagration which followed the destruction of the Temple. Some of the inhabitants escaped, but others met their deaths under the collapsing roofs. In the "burnt house" a man was found still holding his spear. Most of the wooden parts of the furniture and implements were consumed by the flames, but whatever was made of stone or clay survived. In this way, much has been learnt about the daily life of Jerusalemite families on the eve of the destruction of the Second Temple.

Jerusalem, sacred to three religions, has been the cause of unending controversy. Since its foundation by King David some 3,000 years ago, the city has never been abandoned, and each new city has been built on the ruins of the previous one. Despite the great interest in its past, little is known of it archaeologically. Only since 1967 have teams of Israeli archaeologists begun to unfold its secrets. In this photograph one may see the large-scale excavations made at the southern wall of the Temple Mount. Here remains of the Crusader period covered an excellently preserved early Moslem palace constructed over a huge building of the Byzantine period, which in turn covered the remains of Aelia Capitolina, under which the monumental street and stairs leading up to the southern gates of the sacred precinct were discovered. Further up, to the west of the Temple Mount, there came to light the remains of private dwellings, from which come these fragments of painted plaster, resembling multicolored marble or architectural designs.

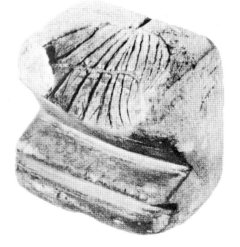

The service of the Temple was a complicated matter. different occasions demanded different rituals. Sacrificial victims ranged from doves to bulls, and there were offerings of various foodstuffs. These inscriptions (Bottom r) were engraved on vessels in which offerings were made, the word *korban* meaning 'sacrifice'. As the prayers, offerings and sacrifices were made at specified times during the day, a time-piece (Bottom l) was a necessary implement.

The Temple was served also by singers and musicians. This Hebrew inscription (L) on stone from walls of the Temple Mount: "To the place of trumpetting . . ." (Herodian period), found in recent excavations, possibly directed the priests to their posts.

◀

A large number of inscriptions in ancient Hebrew, Greek, Aramaic, Latin, Arabic and many other languages have been found in Jerusalem. However, this number diminishes as we move to earlier periods than the late Roman.

About 100 years ago one of the most interesting inscriptions was discovered in Jerusalem (R). This was a Greek text dating to the time when the Temple stood in its full splendor. Then came a rare occurrence. During the construction of a new road in 1935 in the vicinity of St Stephen's Gate, a large fragment of an identical text, written by a different hand, was found. The complete text reads: "An alien should not enter within the limits of the balustrade surrounding the Temple and its court. Whoever is caught doing so will be charged and sentenced to death." Josephus Flavius, himself a priest in the service of the Temple, relates: "Such was the first court. Within it and not far distant was a second one, accessible by a few steps and surrounded by a stone balustrade with an inscription prohibiting the entrance of a foreigner under the threat of the penalty of death." (*Jewish Antiquities 15:417*). The letters in these inscriptions were painted in red, so that the warning should be visible from afar.

Samaria (L), the Israelite capital, was destroyed by the Assyrians in 722 BC. The Assyrians settled foreign peoples there who later received the name Samaritans. Alexander the Great founded a Macedonian colony there. At that time the acropolis of Samaria was surrounded by a wall, strengthened by round towers. The Hasmoneans conquered the city and breached the wall. Herod rebuilt the city and renamed it Sebaste, in honor of Caesar Augustus, his benefactor, constructing there a temple dedicated to the cult of the emperor. At that time Samaria was growing in size and a larger city was built at the foot of the ancient acropolis. On the slope of the acropolis a theater was constructed, and further down a forum. The entire new city was surrounded by a wall, and a new gate, defended by massive round towers, was constructed, from which led a colonnaded street, lined with shops on either sides.

Herodium (R) is one of the fortified palaces which Herod built along the borders of the country, and this is how it was described by Josephus Flavius, the Jewish historian: "Thus he built a fortress on the hills on the Arabian border and called it after himself, Herodium. . . . (*Jewish War I I:419*). Much of what Josephus saw in his time has been uncovered at Herodium, on an isolated hill overlooking the Judean desert to the east and the Holy City to the north.

Mattityah Antigonus (40–37 BC) was the last Hasmonean ruler. In the year of his accession to the throne the Parthians invaded the Holy Land, devastating numerous areas. In 37 BC, Jerusalem was besieged by Herod the Great, whose kingship had been confirmed earlier in Rome. The city was conquered and Hasmonean rule came to an end. The coins of Mattityah (Above) are bilingual. The title of the High Priest, in ancient Hebrew script, was on the obverse, while the reverse bore the title 'king' in Greek. Among the symbols are a wreath and horns of plenty, appearing also on the coins of other Hasmonean rulers.

The anchor, war galley and the horns of plenty, symbols which figured also on Hasmonean coins, were employed by Herod the Great (Above, Bronze, 37 BC, The 3rd year of Herod's reign), in his coinage alongside symbols which would be offensive to his Jewish subjects. Among these latter there was the helmet of the Dioscuri (son of Zeus), the caduceus (the symbol of Hermes), and the tripod (of incense, in pagan temples). It would seem therefore that Herod struck different coins for the use of the Jewish and non-Jewish regions of his large kingdom.

Whereas most of the Roman procurators of the province of Judea were careful not to hurt the religious feelings of their Jewish subjects by minting coins with offensive pagan symbols, Pontius Pilate embarked on a different minting policy. On his coins occur implements employed in pagan cults, such as the simpulum, the ritual laddel which occurs on the reverse side of a coin on the obverse of which are three ears of barley, shown here. This coin was struck in the 18th year of Tiberius, 29–30 AD. The legend reads: *IOYLIA KAICAROC,* Empress Julia, mother of Tiberius.

A drastic change in the policy of minting occurred during the years 66 to 70 AD, during the Jewish War. When the Temple still stood, dues were paid in silver, normally in Tyrian shekels (i.e. tetradrachms) (Overleaf). These, together with a few coins of the Jewish War, were acquired together with the bronze pyxis in Jerusalem. Once the Jewish War broke out the Jewish authorities refrained from using foreign currency, replacing it by independent issues of a quarter, a half and a full shekel. The inscriptions were in ancient, antiquated Hebrew, and the symbols consisted of the chalice, amphora, vine leaf and pomegranate.

Caesarea, founded by Herod as a rival to Jerusalem, was provided with every luxury of the Augustan Age, including running water brought from afar by this high level aqueduct, some 17 km long. The water was first transported in a subterranean conduit from springs at the foot of Mount Carmel to the north. It was then carried over a marsh by means of an arched aqueduct, and again in a tunnel through the low hills running parallel to the coast. Along the sea shore as far as Caesarea, the water was again carried by means of an aqueduct. A large number of inscriptions found along the course of the aqueduct tell of extensive repairs made during the time of Hadrian.

83

The site of kh Qumran, identified with the biblical 'Ir Melah', was known for more than a century, but it was only after the discovery of the Dead Sea Scrolls in caves lying beneath the ancient site, that attention was drawn to the site as well. After a trial dig in 1951, the site was extensively excavated in the years 1953–1956. kh Qumran overlooks the northwestern shores of the Dead Sea. It is situated on a plateau 430 m below sea-level, some 50 m above the Dead Sea. The earliest remains on the site go back to the Iron Age, when an Israelite town existed there in the 8th to 6th centuries BC. It was then settled in the time of John Hyrcanus (135–104 BC). These settlers have been identified by historians as the Essenes, although other scholars prefer an identification with a less specifically defined Dead Sea Sect. In a later stage of the same Hellenistic period, the 80×88 m compound of the sect was built. This in fact was a single large building defended by a massive three-storey-high tower, which protected the main entrance to the compound. There were two large reservoirs within the compound, and several others in the annexes. The only source of water in this region is the scanty rain, collected by channels. Within the compound there were lodgings for members of the sect, a refectory which served also as an assembly hall, and, most important, the scribes' hall in which were found clay tablets and inkstands. Storerooms and workshops were located in an annex to the west of the compound, while to the south there was a large potter's workshop, in which were produced vessels for daily use as well as the large jars in which were kept the scrolls written by the sages and copied by the scribes of the sect. The site was abandoned in about the 4th century BC and finally destroyed in the summer of 68 AD during the Jewish War.

With the publication of the documents found at Qumran there were also published fragments of the biblical excerpts included in the phylacteries (*Tefilin*). However, it was only with the late appearance of this set of phylacteries, worn on the head, that a complete object of this class has come to light. It measures only 20×13 mm., and is made of calf's skin, in which were wrapped four minute scrolls each containing a passage from the Pentateuch: Ex. 13:1–10, Deut. 6:4–9, Ex. 13:11–16 and Deut. 11:13–21. This still remains a unique object in its class.

The Isaiah scroll. In 1947 a Bedouin shepherd stumbled on an old jar, and made history. It happened in a cave in the vicinity of kh Qumran, which, since then, has become one of the most famous places in the world. In that place there lived in sanctity a small sect, whose scribes were engaged in copying out the Holy Scriptures, their sages in writing commentaries on the books of the Bible and on the writings which had been left out of the official Bible, and the leaders of the sect were occupied in laying down the rules for a future kingdom in which righteousness would reign. The biblical books, to which this Isaiah scroll belongs, are of special importance. Firstly, they antedate by 1,000 years any other extant copy of the Bible; secondly, since they belong to the period when the codification of the Bible was taking place, they serve as a unique source for learning how the codification was accomplished.

Of no less interest are the commentaries on the books of the Bible and on the Apocrypha found at Qumran. All of these books were written by sages of the Dead Sea sect, and reflect sources of learning otherwise unknown to us. Of some of the commentaries, such as the ones on Psalms, Isaiah, Michah, Zephaniah and Nahum only fragments have been found, but of Habbakuk, to which this scroll belongs, most of the book is extant. In some of these commentaries oral traditions which are never mentioned in any other sources were recorded in writing. In the same way, we are able to derive considerable knowledge concerning the history of the sect, its origins, and the actions of its leader, the Teacher of Righteousness.

Masada is a natural-rock stronghold on the western shore of the Dead Sea. One of the early Hasmonean rulers used this site as a stronghold on the eastern frontier of Judea. In the year 40 BC, on the point of leaving for home to seek confirmation of his kingship, Herod left his family here. On his return as king, he began to build the fortress, which Josephus Flavius describes in great detail: "First he enclosed the entire summit, a circuit measuring seven furlongs, with a wall of white stone . . . ; on it stood 37 towers 50 cubits high, from which access was obtained to the apartments constructed round the whole interior of the wall . . . . There, too, he built a palace on the western slope, beneath the ramparts on the crest and inclining towards the north . . . . The fittings of the interior — apartments, colonnades, and bath — were of manifold variety and sumptuous; . . . But the stores laid up within would have excited still more amazement, alike for their lavish splendor and their durability . . . ." (*Jewish War 7:280–300*). The excavations of Masada in 1963–1965 affirmed just how accurately Josephus had described Masada.

During the revolt the coins bear designs and motifs connected with the Temple in Jerusalem. In this silver tetradrachm is represented the Temple Façade with four columns.

When the Bar Kohbah revolt took place (132–135 AD), Masada was deserted. The insurgents in this part of Judea concentrated around Engeddi, whose oasis supplied food for the soldiers and their families. When that place was conquered, the remnants of the rebels found refuge in caves to the north and south of the oasis. They took with them their most precious belongings, spoil which they had taken from Roman soldiers, the keys of their houses, to which they were never to return, and documents, mostly personal, but also including the archives of the leaders of the revolt. One of these documents is a letter from Shimeon, the leader of the revolt, to Joshua son of Galgala, one of his subordinates (Bottom r).

Archaeology is a science dealing with the remains of material culture: flints, potsherds, temples, gates, coins; it is rare for an archaeologist to become emotionally involved in his finds. One of these cases is when he stumbles on finds like these at Masada, pertaining to one of the almost 1,000 men, women and children who met their tragic end here on the first day of May 73 AD. These finds (Overleaf l) included a woman's mirror, bone spindle whorls and buttons, and bundles of unknitted wool. It is this kind of find which brings the archaeologist close to the object of his research: man.

90 | 91 | 92 | 93

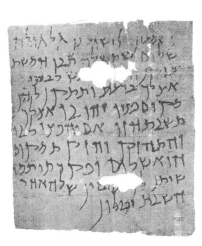

The large necropolis of Beth Shearim near the small Jewish town of the same name, is situated in the southern foothills of Lower Galilee. It prospered mainly from the 2nd century AD, when the balance of Jewish settlement shifted from devastated Judea to Galilee. The special attraction of the necropolis of Beth Shearim is the burial cave of Rabbi Judah the Patriarch, the spiritual leader of local Jewry, and the codifier of the *Mishnah,* the basis of Jewish law. Jews were brought here from all over the Holy Land and from many countries in the Diaspora, from as far as South Arabia to Palmyra and Phoenicia. Many of the tombs were decorated, mostly by local artists, and some by relatives of the deceased. For the most part, Jewish symbols were employed. The menorah became prominent, but there were also other elements used. Quite often there were carved images of humans and animals, which attest to the radical change which Jews underwent after the destruction of the Temple, a process of which we shall become more aware in reviewing synagogal art.

During the excavations of the large theater at Caesarea a most curious find was made. The theater was constructed by the founder of the city, Herod the Great, who introduced this purely Roman institution into the Holy Land, alongside with other novelties imported from Rome. An unusual feature of this theater, however, was a series of 14 floors made of plaster, each replacing the previous one damaged by wear. The floors were painted in patterns resembling marble. Constant use of the theater over a century, made it necessary to consolidate the structure, and a semi-circular *exedra* was added at the back of the theater. A change of taste in the later Roman period prescribed the adaptation of the structure to water games. During this period — the 3rd–4th centuries AD — repairs were also made in the rows of seats, making use of stones from older buildings which had fallen into disuse. One of these stones was inscribed: TIBERIEUM — PONTIUS POILATUS — PREFECTUS IUDAEAE. This stone came from a building which Pontius Pilate, the governor of Judea, dedicated to the Emperor Tiberius. *Sic transit gloria mundi (et Hominum)* . . .

The fortress Antonia. During the time of the First Temple, there had existed a fortress called the Tower of Hananel north of the Temple Mount. After the return from Babylon, the site was again fortified by Nehemia. The Seleucids destroyed this fortification in about 167 BC constructing in its stead the fortress of Baris (the name meaning 'castle'), dominating the Temple. When Herod built the new Temple he also constructed a new fortress on the same site, naming it Antonia, in honor of Mark Antony, his friend. After the king's death the Romans posted a garrison there. Josephus (*Jewish War 5:244*) describes this fortress as a large fortified palace, with a strong tower in the middle, and four towers in the corners, the southeastern of which was 70 cubits high. It was built high so that the Temple could be viewed from it: "for a Roman cohort was permanently quartered there, and at the festivals, took up positions in arms to watch the people and repress any insurrectionary movement." The entry of Jesus to Jerusalem was certainly regarded as such a movement.

Most scholars identify the site of the Antonia as being on both sides of the present-day Via Dolorosa, at the section opposite the northwestern part of the Temple Mount. The stone seen here belongs to the pavement of a street, or court, discovered below the convent of the Sisters of Zion, identified as the *lithostrotos,* or 'paved court'. The scratchings on the stones (R) are believed to be connected with games played by Roman soldiers who were posted in the fortress.

This griffin from Erez, to the south of the coastal plain, is of the later Roman period and is one of the latest specimens of this kind of art. According to Herodotus, griffins were the guardians of gold somewhere at the northern end of the world. It is uncertain whether the Greeks considered the griffin an animal or a bird. Griffins became a much favored subject in the art of the Hellenistic period, and have always been described as winged creatures, rather like the cherubim and sphinxes of ancient times. The griffin, singly or in pairs, is always depicted with one leg resting on a wheel.

The theater at Beth Shean (R), a completely artificial structure of the Roman style, situated to the west of the ancient mound which formed part of the beautiful background, is the best preserved in the Holy Land. It was constructed in the 2nd century AD. The theater is 90 m long, seating some 8,000 spectators. During the late Roman period the theater was adapted for water games, like the theater at Caesarea. In contrast to the latter, whose decoration was basically floral, that of Beth Shean included comic and tragic masks, as well as friezes in which were portrayed animals, both real and imaginary. In the Byzantine period dice was played in the theater.

97 | 98

To the north of the small Canaanite and Philistine Ashkelon a large metropolis began to grow in the Persian period. At the beginning of this period it became a Tyrian harbor and contained a large palace. During the reign of the Ptolemies, in 111 BC it achieved independence, with the right of minting silver money. Herod the Great was born there, and in gratitude he constructed toward the end of his life, temples, palaces, and a large stoa. The town was raised to the status of a Colony under the Romans. As such it attracted numerous philosophers and grammarians. Although Greek in its culture, a large Jewish community lived at Ashkelon. Among the deities venerated at Ashkelon were Atargatis-Derketo, Isis, Apollo and Hercules. It also housed one of the three largest markets in the Holy Land. To the Byzantine period belong numerous churches and one synagogue. Although the mound, covering only 15 acres, has been extensively excavated, the later city remains almost unexplored. The only building which has been investigated is a 110 m long structure, which housed the council-house. It consisted of a huge open-air courtyard surrounded by porticos, and terminating in a large apse at its southern end, the seat of the councilors. It also housed a small temple to Apollo. To the north of the building there was a court 37×57 m in size. Along the hall of the council-house were lined large reliefs made of marble, depicting winged victories, holding a wreath in their right hand and a palm branch in their left. The victories stand on globes, each of which is carried by Atlas. There were few other remains of the Roman period found on this site, which once boasted temples and palaces.

This inscription (R) was engraved on a stone in the 15th course of the Western Wall of the Temple Mount, just to the south of the Wailing Wall. The man who wrote the inscription had in mind *Isaiah 66:14* which reads: "You shall see, and your heart shall rejoice; your bones shall florish like the grass." The verse which precedes it is: "and you shall find comfort in Jerusalem." This inscription is dated by the excavator to the time of Julian (362 AD), who attempted to rebuild the Jewish Temple in Jerusalem.

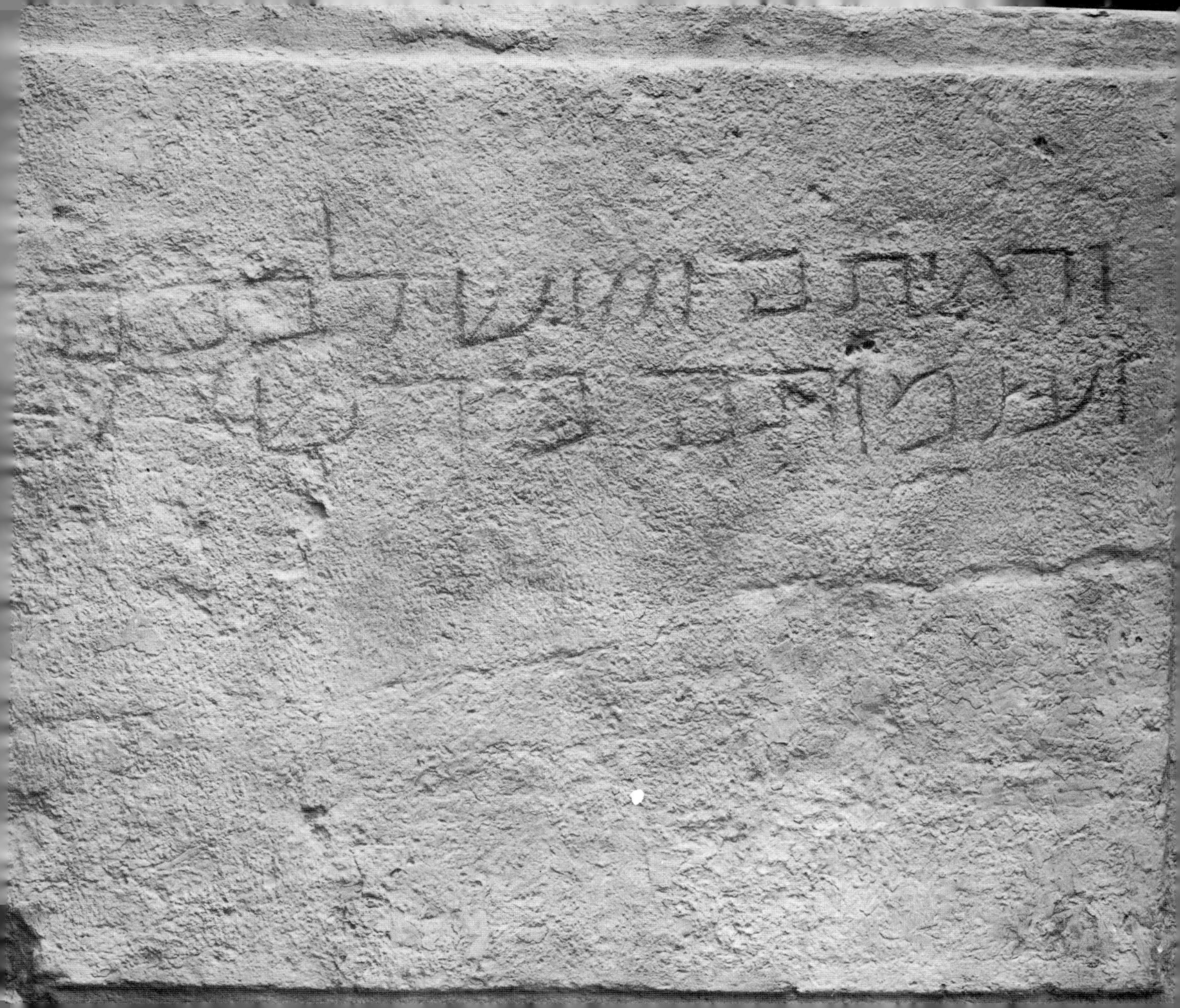

Following his victory over Licinius in 324 AD Emperor Constantine embarked on a plan to make Jerusalem the Holy City of Christianity. Macarius, the bishop of Aelia induced the emperor and Helene, his mother, to clear the sepulchre of Jesus of the heaps of rubbish which covered it and to build a church there. In the course of the next two centuries the Holy City was practically covered by churches and monasteries. Churches and chapels were built on all the sites associated with the martyrdom of Jesus and the acts of his disciples. Apart from these religious buildings, a large number of inns and baths were also built to accommodate the Christian pilgrims who thronged the streets of Jerusalem.

Several large buildings, parts of which stand three stories high, were recently discovered at the excavations south of the southern wall of the Temple Mount. These buildings were erected at the time of Constantine, damaged during the reign of Julian the Apostate and repaired after his death. These buildings probably served as inns for the accommodation of Christian pilgrims, one of whom engraved a cross on one of the stones in the nearby wall.

During the thousands of years of its history, the Holy Land has changed its name several times, and scores of times changed its internal administrative and territorial divisions. From being part of a Persian satrapy, it became a part of the Ptolemaic kingdom; the Seleucids broke it up into about ten independent districts. By the end of the Hasmonean rule most of the Holy Land was united into one kingdom, but the Romans in 63 BC curtailed the Judean kingdom and began to break it up into independent city territories. Herod halted this process for some time, but after his death it gained momentum, each city territory belonging to a Roman provincial government, either the province of Syria or of Judea. The tendency in the late Roman and Byzantine period was to form larger administrative units. In the beginning, Palestine was divided into two such units, Prima and Salutaris, i.e., 'First' and 'Last', to the north and south of Beersheba. In 429, this twofold division became triple, 'First', 'Second', and 'Third'. This inscription is a large fragment, one of several, found at Beersheba, and lists the tax regulations of Palestina Tertia. On the left are names of cities, mostly in the section of the province east of the *Arabah,* in the middle are listed the amounts to be paid, while in the broken off part were written additional amounts to be paid for the upkeep of the local provincial administration. This important document dates from the 5th century AD.

The earliest known geographical description of the Land of the Bible is the Madabah map, based on sources dating back to the 4th century AD. Madabah was a biblical town in the land of Moab to the east of the Dead Sea. In the Hellenistic period it was conquered by the Hasmoneans, but was ceded by them to the Nabateans, the neighbors of Judea in the Roman period. It formed part of the Provincia Arabia after 106 AD, and by the 4th century it had become an important Christian town. In the course of two or three centuries, ten churches were built in this town, two of which were dedicated to Mary Mother of God and to the prophet Elijah respectively. Two of the churches have been excavated, and in both were discovered beautiful mosaic pavements. Of more importance was the church situated in the vicinity of the northern gate at which this floor was found, dating from the 6th century AD. It was discovered in 1884, when a new Orthodox church was built on its site. The map, 25×7.5 m in size, decorated the transept of the basilica. It depicts the land extending from Phoenicia in the north to as far south as Thebes in Egypt. At the center of the map is located Jerusalem, with some details of the city marked, including the cardo, the main street, running from the northern gate (the Damascus Gate of today), lined with colonnades, the church of the Holy Sepulchre and various other important ecclesiastical buildings. Above, to the east, is the Dead Sea on which are sailing two boats carrying salt. The sailors here were mutilated by iconoclasts during some later period, but still under Christian rule, as is indicated by the repairs made. Further east are the mountains of Moab. Southeast of the Dead Sea can be seen the oasis of Zoara, a fortified city surrounded by palm groves. To the left, north of the Sea, is the River Jordan, showing fishes turning back at the bitter taste of the water. To the north, west, and south of Jerusalem are written in larger letters the names of the tribes Dan, Judah, and Simeon. The larger cities are depicted in more detail, whereas the smaller towns, villages and sites of biblical importance are symbolized by representative features, and described by appropriate biblical quotations. There are very few sources of such importance as this map for the study of the ancient historical-geography of the Holy Land.

103

In 732 BC the kingdom of Israel was conquered by the Assyrians who "brought people from Babylon, Cuthah, Avva, Hammath, and Sepharvaim, and settled them in the cities of Samaria in place of the Israelites; so they occupied Samaria and lived in its cities . . . . The king of Assyria, therefore, gave orders that one of the priests deported from Samaria should be sent back to live there and teach the people the usage of the god of the country." (*II Kings 18:24ff*). From that time throughout the Persian, Hellenistic, Roman, and Byzantine periods the Samaritans occupied territory bordered on the north by the Valley of Jezreel, Judea on the south, the Jordan to the east and the coastal plain to the west. At quite an early date the Samaritans accepted the Hebrew Pentateuch, into which they introduced slight changes. The Samaritans did not, however, accept the oral teachings (the Mishnah and the Talmud) and hence arose the main difference between the Jews and the Samaritans, a source of enmity which abated only after the foundation of the modern State of Israel. Archaeological research has hardly touched on the Samaritans. Samaritan traditions, none earlier than the 4th century AD, name numerous synagogues in the region of which the Samaritan holy mountain, Mount Gerizim, forms the center. There has also been discovered a large number of Samaritan inscriptions, amulets, and lamps both in the Samaritan region as well as in places where mixed communities lived. One of these inscriptions is the tablet on which the Ten Commandments were engraved in the Samaritan script, which retained the ancient Hebrew form. This inscription was found at Shaalabim, situated 3 km north of Emmaus, at the southwestern corner of the Samaritan territory. In this place there was a Samaritan synagogue. The building was designed to face toward Mount Gerizim. It has been identified as Samaritan partly on the basis of a Samaritan inscription, and dates from the 4th or 5th century AD.

Very little remains of the mosaic floor of the Samaritan synagogue of Shaalabim. On the partly preserved medallion are seen two menoroth, not of the regular seven-branched type found in contemporary Jewish art, but of an indeterminate number of branches. Between the menoroth is a triangular object, which is believed to represent Mt Gerizim. The fragmentary Greek inscription possibly refers to the renewing of the mosaic pavement. Another inscription, in Samaritan, reads: "The Lord shall reign for ever and for ever" (Ex. 15:18).

The synagogue at Engeddi is one of the most recent discoveries in the holy Land. In the excavations of 1970–1972 two superimposed synagogues were discovered, the earlier of the late 2nd to early 3rd century AD and the latter form the 5th–6th centuries. The lower building was 12.5×13.5 m, a basilical building, of which the mosaic floor was discovered intact. This synagogue is unique in the austerity of its decoration, differing from all those known hitherto. The main hall has a carpet of intersecting circles with a crow-step border. In the center of the carpet is a medallion within a lozenge, within a square. There are two pairs of birds in the middle and four pairs of peacocks in the corners. On the dais there is a bird within a circle, close to which two small bronze menoroth were found. In the western aisle there are five Hebrew and Aramaic inscriptions. The first quotes *I Chron. 1:1–4*: "Adam, Seth, Enosh, Kenan, Mahalalel, Jared, Enoch, Methusaleh, Lamech, Noah (the sons of Noah) Shem, Ham, Japhet." The second inscription has the names of the 12 signs of the zodiac and of the 12 months of the year, ending with the names of the Patriarchs and the three companions of Daniel, and with the blessing "Peace be on Israel." The third inscription mentions the donors, and curses men who commit certain sins against the community. The fourth inscription refers to the man who built the "great steps", while the last bestows a blessing on all the people of the town who helped renovate the synagogue.

Susiye, the little-known site, the scene of some very important discoveries, is situated northwest of Eshtemoa, at which a better known synagogue was discovered. This site has been in the process of excavation since 1970. It lies in the heart of the mountains of Hebron, a region where Jewish settlement persisted throughout the Jewish War at the outbreak of which Jews were expelled from the territory of Jerusalem, as they were during the cruel persecution which followed the Bar Kohbah revolt. At Susiye (this Arab name possibly reflects an ancient Hebrew form) no less than four phases of construction of synagogues dating from the 4th to the 9th century AD have been observed. It was only after the 9th century that a Moslem mosque was built on the site of the synagogue. The most interesting phase in the existence of the synagogue is that of the 4th century, to which belongs the beautiful mosaic pavement (Above). Originally this floor, too, consisted of three panels, for there is evidence that a panel of zodiacal symbols once existed. Fully preserved is the representation of the Torah Shrine, made in the form of a gabled building in the middle of which stands the Shrine itself. At the sides of the shrine stand two menoroth, each flanked by ritual implements. Numerous inscriptions were found, pertaining to the various phases. The results of these excavations have not yet been published.

Kefar Baram was a Jewish town in Upper Galilee, 11 km northwest of Safed. This settlement was not abandoned until the middle of the 18th century. This site is known by its Arabic name only, which most probably retained the ancient Hebrew form. It is one of the very few settlements which was never mentioned in ancient sources, the earliest being by Jewish pilgrims from the 13th century onward, who mention the Jewish community there and its synagogue. There were two synagogues at Kefar Baram, one of which has vanished since the last century. The other synagogue, the larger of the two, is of the Galilean type, situated at the highest point in the town (R). The 20×15.20 m building was built of excellent ashlars. It has a porch in front of the façade, an element unique in this type of synagogue. The three entrances face toward Jerusalem. In the interior, there are three colonnades with benches along the wall. Like most synagogues in the Galilee this building, too, was built of the hard, yellowish local limestone. The three entrances were framed by Roman style decoration and the lintel of the main door is decorated by two victories supporting a wreath. Over one window there is the following inscription: "Built by Eleazar, son of Yudan."

Chorazin was one of the three cities reproached by Jesus for failing to accept his teaching (*Matthew 11:20–24; Luke 10:12–16*). Eusebius in the 4th century AD mentions it as a ruined city. In its present state the city is from the 2nd and 3rd centuries AD. The most important building in the city is the partly excavated synagogue. It is 23×17 m in size, a building with three entrances facing south, toward Jerusalem. The roof of the building was originally supported by three colonnades. There were benches along three sides of the prayer-hall, for seating the community. The building, of which only the foundations and the floor were preserved, was of hard black basalt. Of particular interest is the architectural decoration. It is provincial-Roman, and its makers did not refrain from sculpting human figures and animals. The stone chair (L) has a memorial inscription engraved on it: "May Yudan, the son of Ishmael, be remembered for good, who made this stoa and its staircase. As his reward may he have a share with the righteous." This is possibly the Seat of Moses mentioned in the New Testament (*Matthew 23:2*), possibly intended for an elder of the community.

Two types of synagogue were built in the Holy land, the Galilean type — ashlar buildings with architectural decoration, represented by the synagogue of Chorazin and others, and the slightly later type of synagogue decorated by mosaic, and of inferior construction. To the later type belongs the 5th–6th century synagogue of Beth Alpha. Whereas the decoration of the Galilean type follows pagan prototypes, the mosaic is didactic. The mosaic floor was divided into three sections. At the entrance a biblical story was told, the main theme of which was salvation by the hand of God: Daniel in the lions' den, Noah's Ark and the sacrifice of Isaac (Above). The story begins on the left where the two servants of Abraham are told to wait with the beast. Then the ram is seen with its horns entangled in the bush ("and here is a ram" says the inscription above). Above the bush is the hand of God emerging from heaven, symbolized by palm trees ("do not touch"). Abraham is holding Isaac in his hands in front of the altar on which the wood is already burning.

The second panel contains the heavenly chariot of Helios, the Greek sun-god, the 12 symbols of the zodiac, and, in the corners, the four seasons of the year. The Torah shrine flanked by two monoroth, forms the third panel, close to the dais. This scheme was followed in several synagogues. The floor was made by a father and son, Marianos and Haninah, during the reign of Justin.

Hammath, the site of the famous ancient hot springs, and Tiberias, were originally two separate towns. Perhaps by the 1st century AD both localities became united within a single wall. Two synagogues were discoverd at Hammath. One was excavated in 1921, and was in fact the first archaeological excavation made by Jewish archaeologists in the Holy Land. The second synagogue was excavated in the years 1961–1963. This beautiful spot is situated at a distance of only 150 m from the Sea of Galilee. There were three main phases of construction on this site. To the earliest phase, of the late 1st to early 2nd century AD, is attributed a large building identified as a gymnasium, or perhaps a synagogue (we do not know what synagogues looked like in that period). In the 4th century this building was replaced by a synagogue, to which this mosaic floor belongs. This building was of the broadhouse type, 15×13 m in size, entered from the south. The aisles were decorated by purely geometrical carpets. At the southern end of the main hall there were six dedicatory inscriptions flanked by two lions. The inscriptions, in Greek, mentioned donors and officials responsible for the construction of the synagogue (the names of these were Severus, Julius, Profuturus, attesting to the extent of assimilation which affected this rich Jewish community). The main panel depicts Helios riding in his celestial chariot against a background of the Sun, Moon, and stars (this part of the pavement is still masked by a wall from a later period). The Helios scene is surrounded by the 12 signs of the zodiac, each symbol identified by its name in Hebrew, and also by the four seasons of the year. Close to the dais the Torah Shrine is depicted flanked by two menoroth. At the sides of the menoroth are an incense shovel, a shophar, (ram's horn) and a *lulav* and *etrog*. Although there is nothing specifically new in this composition, artistically it is the best to have survived. It was possibly constructed by an artist who came from one of the international centers, perhaps from Antioch in Syria, a metropolis for mosaic-makers at that time. This synagogue was repaired, and changes introduced at various periods until the 8th century AD.

Early Christian art at the Church at Shavei Zion. This site, on which a church was discovered in 1955, is situated 7 km north of Acre. Although most of the superstructure of the building has long vanished, the two superimposed mosaic pavements attest to a rather long history. To the earlier phase, dating possibly to the fourth century AD, belong depictions of large crosses, one of which is shown here. It is flanked by two pomegranates below which are two fishes, a symbol quite common in early Christian art of the Holy Land. This floor was covered in a later phase by a second mosaic pavement, dated by a dedicatory inscription to 485/86 AD. The decoration of this later floor consists of rich geometric patterns only. It thus confirms that the ban issued by Theodosius II in 427 AD on the representation of crosses in floors was observed in the Holy Land.

This site was named *Heptapegon*, which means in Greek 'the land of Seven Springs'. It is situated on the western shore of the Sea of Galilee, north of Capernaum. Aetheria, a pilgrim, visited the site at the end of the 4th century AD, mentioning a chapel commemorating the miracle of the Loaves and Fishes. From the early 6th century the place was much frequented by Christian pilgrims. In excavations on the site, remains of a 4th century chapel, and of a large church built above it in the latter part of the same century, have been uncovered. This was a 25×19 m building decorated with mosaics. At the dais, the *mensa christi,* at which the miracle was performed, is shown. Part of the mosaics of the nave have been preserved, showing a view with water fowl, trees, and marshes. At the entrance to the dais is a small panel portraying a basket with loaves of bread marked with crosses and flanked by two fishes.

Capernaum, a small Jewish town, was situated on the western shore of the Sea of Galilee and was important in the development of early Christianity. According to the New Testament a Roman centurion built a synagogue there (*Luke 7:2–5*). Jesus preached there and performed miracles (*Matthew 9:5–34, etc.*), and as the city would not listen to his preaching, he cursed it (*Matthew 11:23–24*). At the beginning of the 2nd century AD a Jewish-Christian community existed there. In recent excavations a house from the 1st century AD has been uncovered, identified as the house of St Peter, which served as an early Christian prayer-house. The synagogue (L) is one of the best preserved buildings in the Holy Land. Recent excavations, which are still in progress, indicate that it was erected (or rebuilt completely from the foundations) in the late 4th or early 5th century AD, and not in the 2nd or 3rd as was previously believed.

115 | 116

The large monastery of the Virgin Mary was erected on the lower slope of the ancient mound of Beth Shean. It was decorated by totally "un-Christian" mosaics. One of the rooms has a beautiful vintage scene, while the main hall has in the center of a large carpet a medallion with Helios and Selene (moon). Around it are the 12 months represented by women clad according to the season of the year. The rest of the pavement is full of small rhomboids containing fruits, birds, animals, a hunter and an animal hit by an arrow. The monastery dates from about 567 AD.

| 117

1772

The Good Shepherd of Caesarea Maritima. As in the Roman period, Christian Caesarea was the great rival of Jerusalem for supremacy in the Holy Land. This city had a bishop as early as the end of the 2nd century AD. In the 3rd and 4th centuries AD Origen and Eusebius, two Fathers of the Christian Church, taught in the famous school of Caesarea, in the large library of which was made the famous translation of the Bible, known as the Hexapla, on account of the six columns in which it was made. Since the early 1960s of our century numerous Christian buildings have been unearthed. In one of these, situated to the south of the later date Crusader moat, perhaps the famous library itself, was discovered a statue of Jesus, represented as the Good Shepherd. He carries the lamb on his shoulder, while at his feet are the remains of the four legs of another lamb, and of the edge of the *pedum,* the shepherd's staff. This statue probably dates to the 4th or 5th centuries AD.

Christian monasticism began in the Holy Land during the 4th century AD. In the beginning hermits lived alone in secluded caves in the desert, in the vicinity of a source of water. In time the single hermit was followed by his friends and companions, who lived in nearby caves. In this way sprang up the laurae. These caves and small cells were later replaced by larger buildings. This picture depicts the earliest laura, founded by St Khareitun in 334 AD at Faran, near Jerusalem.

| 119

Avdat (Obodoa) (R) is situated in the center of the mountains of the Negev. It is one of the six towns which flourished there from the Hellenistic period to the Arab conquest of the Holy Land. The town was founded by Nabateans, an Arabian tribe which by the late Roman period had lost its Semitic language and script, and by the 4th century AD had begun to convert to Christianity. In each of these towns two or three churches were built, some of which were attached to monasteries. At Obodoa two churches were built on the acropolis, where there once stood a Nabatean and a late Roman temple. The earliest church is from the 4th century AD, and the other, the Church of St Theodore, dates from a century later. In the background is seen the large late Roman-Byzantine citadel.

| 120

The isolated early Moslem palace of Khirbet el Mefjer is located amidst flourishing orchards 2 km north of Jericho. Its construction was begun by Abd el Malik in 724–743 AD, but was never completed, due to an earthquake which shattered it in 746 AD. It was a huge rectangular building two stories high, with higher towers at the four corners. A magnificent gateway led to a spacious court around which were numerous guest rooms, a large mosque, a beautiful small *diwan,* a large bath and a huge decorative pool. The mosque, the *diwan* and certain other rooms were decorated with mosaics, and the walls and ceilings were covered in sculptures of gypsum. The sculpture shows a remarkable blend of eastern and western influences.

The Dome of the Rock, erroneously named the Mosque of Omar by Europeans (R), was built by Abd el Malik Ibn Marwan in 691 AD, some 50 years after the Arab conquest of the Holy Land. The Dome, constructed on the traditional site of Mount Moriah, from which Mohammad allegedly ascended to Heaven, was built of materials taken from the large Christian churches, destroyed by the Persians in 614 AD. The building was repaired in the 9th century by the Abbasid Caliph el Mamun, who replaced the original dedication by his own, forgetting, however, to replace the date as well. The Crusaders transformed this building into a *Templum Domini,* replacing the crescent at the top of the roof by a large golden cross. This was changed back by Saladin in 1187. The plan of the building is that of a circle inscribed within an octagon, and surmounted by a dome. The arches and the walls are all covered by mosaics of rich floral design, which are not free of Byzantine influence. Verses of the Koran are interlaced in the mosaics.

Nazareth was a small Jewish town in Lower Galilee where Jesus was raised and where Mary and Joseph lived. In his youth Jesus preached in the local synagogue, but the Jews refused to listen to him. It remained a Jewish town in later centuries, too, the Christians finding it difficult to build churches there. It was in fact not until the 6th century AD that the first Christian church was built there. During the Crusader period, Nazareth was an important religious center. The Archibishop had his residence there, and monasteries and churches were built in the city. The most elaborate Crusader church was built over the site of the Cave of the Annunciation in the style of that period, the 12th century. That building, too, vanished almost completely, except for the capitals which adorned it. The carvings depict scenes from the life and acts of the apostles. In this capital St Thomas is seen together with the other apostles. It was produced a short time before the crucial battle of Horns of Hittin (1187), after which the Crusaders lost most of the country, including Nazareth, to the Moslems.

The church of St Anne in Jerusalem, although not the largest, is the best preserved church in the Holy Land. It was built by the Crusaders in the 12th century, close to the Pool of Bethesda, replacing an older church from the Byzantine period. The building is 34×19.5 m in size. The interior decoration of the building is sparing and very austere.

The lintel of the Church of the Holy Sepulchre forms part of a lintel placed by the Crusaders above the new entrance which they made to the Church of the Holy Sepulchre. It is composed of two parts, each by a different artist. On it are depicted scenes from the life of Jesus before his Crucifixion. There are five scenes: the resurrection of Lazarus (the first two scenes of which do not appear here), the preparation of the Paschal Lamb, the entry of Jesus into Jerusalem (damaged). The people seen above the damaged portion represent the crowds applauding Jesus with joyful shouts of "Hosanna". The last scene, on the right, depicts the Last Supper. It is framed within three arches. Jesus and the disciples are seated at a curved table, covered by a cloth. In front of the table stands Judas. Jesus is embracing John. This lintel forms one of the most important examples of Crusader art in the Holy Land.

◄

The Church of the Nativity in Bethlehem was constructed by Constantine the Great in 326 AD. It was destroyed during the Samaritan revolt of 529 AD, and subsequently repaired by order of Justinian. Tradition relates that the three Magi saved the church from destruction during the Persian invasion of 614 AD, when hundreds of other churches were set on fire. Since then the church has been in constant use by Christians and repeatedly repaired and altered. By this process, most of the original decoration has vanished. This icon of Mary and the infant Jesus is of a relatively early date.

Kohav Hayarden (Belvoir) is a Crusader border fortress built by the Hospitallers in about the middle of the 12th century AD. It successfully withstood the constant attacks of Saladin, and remained one of the two unconquered fortresses in the Holy Land. It was only in 1191 that the knights were forced to surrender. In 1241 the fortress of Belvoir was destroyed by al Malik al Muazzam. Belvoir occupied the site of a Jewish village by the name of Agrippina, at which beacons were lit to announce the appearance of the new moon.

After a long and arduous march over the Transjordanian plateau in 1116 AD, King Baldwin reached Elath on the Red Sea, also conquering the nearby island of Jazirat Faraun (Pharaoh's Island), which he named Ille de Graye, constructing a citadel there. This conquest was of little importance, because it merely deflected to Mecca the movement of Moslem pilgrims who used to sail by it. Saladin conquered this island in 1187. The present citadel is of much later date.

Acre is one of the earliest cities in the Holy Land and its history reflects the vicissitudes of the country. In 1099 Acre was conquered by the Crusaders, who named it St Jean d'Acre. It was the main Crusader harbor and naval base. Acre quickly developed into a very important economic center, and through it passed the commerce between East and West. The city was divided into several areas, each national community founding its own fortress and headquarters. The hall seen here (Above) was part of the fortress of the Order of the Hospitallers, and was known popularly by the name of the Crypt of St John.

Caesarea, too (R), reflects 1500 years of history in the Holy Land. Although conquered by the Crusaders in 1099, it did not achieve significance until 1254 AD, when Louis IX of France constructed an apparently impregnable fortress extending over an area of 30 acres. These fortifications were, however, soon conquered by the Baibars, who destroyed the city in 1265 AD.

The Lions' Gate (Overleaf) is the only open gate in tthe eastern wall of Jerusalem. It was built in the days of Suleiman the Magnificent, who constructed the walls of Jerusalem in the years 1539–1542. The lions belong to the coat of arms of the Baibars, but are believed to have been placed here by two brothers who were responsible for the construction of the section of the wall extending from the Jaffa Gate to this point. The Lions' Gate is also known as St Mary's Gate, and the Gate of the Tribes, while the Christians call it St Stephen's Gate. This gate symbolizes the fate and history of the Holy City.